D0839735

The purpose of this study guide is to provide supplemental educational material. It is not intended as a substitute or replacement of WHEN MY NAME WAS KEOKO.

Published by SuperSummary, www.supersummary.com

ISBN – 9798648072978

For more information or to learn about our complete library of study guides, please visit http://www.supersummary.com

Please submit any comments, corrections, or questions to:
http://www.supersummary.com/support/

TABLE OF CONTENTS

When My Name Was Keoko (2002) is a young adult work of historical fiction by Linda Sue Park about the Japanese occupation of Korea during World War II. Many praise the novel for how it exposes this often overlooked topic in history, authentically portraying Korean life, culture, and perspective in the 1940s. Park wrote the narrative in alternating chapters from the first-person perspective voices of two Korean siblings: 10-year-old Sun-hee (aka Keoko) and 13-year-old Tae-yul (aka Nobuo). They live with their father (Abuji), mother (Omoni), and Uncle in a small town. The descriptive writing style gives the story the feeling of a personal diary.

Plot Summary

Before Japan enters the war in 1942, Sun-hee and Tae-yul explain the ways in which Korean families must operate and survive during occupation—since Japan invaded Korea decades before the war. Students must speak Japanese, study Japanese, and neglect their Korean roots. It is illegal to speak of, display, or keep any symbol of Korean heritage, and punishable by jail or police beatings. To complicate matters, with the approach of the war, Korea's situation becomes worse. The Japanese begin to enforce more unreasonable laws, including the name change of each resident. Each character must give up their Korean name and select a Japanese one. No one is happy, but they must follow the rules or face punishment. Sun-hee's family chooses a name to secretly reflect their Korean pride (Kaneyama, which honors the gold hidden in Korea's mountains).

Throughout the narrative, Abuji is calm and rational, refusing to resist the Japanese in obvious ways. But Uncle is more rebellious, vocally challenging the unfair laws and becoming involved in a secret Korean resistance as a printmaker to combat the Japanese oppressor. But his life remains in danger by his involvement in his Korean resistance newspaper, and the family grows worried. Meanwhile, as the story progresses, Sun-hee becomes studious and fearlessly confident—even as a young Korean girl whose role is traditionally in the kitchen. She admires her Uncle, and observes his changing attitude as Japanese tyranny takes a stronger hold. She is inquisitive, observant, and supportive, often calculating ways to help her family endure. Her older brother, Tae-yul, equally invests himself in his family's well-being, but since he is a boy, he receives more permission to help his Uncle with small tasks. Both of these young characters show a deep admiration for Uncle, who teaches them about forbidden knowledge, such as how to draw the Korean flag.

When Sun-hee learns about a potentially dangerous situation from her Japanese school friend, she reacts instinctively by alerting her Uncle, knowing he might be at risk of severe punishment. Uncle is grateful, packs his belongings, and flees in secrecy, unable to explain why or where he is going. This act devastates the family, and it marks the beginning of many drastic changes they will all endure for years as Japan's abuse of Koreans during the war escalates. Soon, the Japanese begin to patrol every neighborhood more closely and even invade homes for random searches. The fear and anxiety causes strain in the family, and every character's sense of right or wrong and good or bad becomes warped. Tae-yul grows angry with his father's passivity, and Sun-hee becomes despondent and blames herself for causing Uncle's departure. However, there are small moments of community and trust, such as when Sun-hee and Omoni help Mrs. Ahn, their widowed neighbor, against soldiers during neighborhood searches.

In desperation, and with dwindling supplies and options, Tae-yul—a laborer and plane enthusiast who helped build an airstrip for the war—joins the Japanese Imperial Army to gain his family honor and extra supplies. By this point he is nearly 18, and sees his role in the family as a provider. Inspired by his Uncle's courage, he thrives in training and dedicates himself to becoming a kamikaze pilot. He and Sun-hee develop a secret system of communication since the Japanese censors his letters. At first he seems to be doing very well and has a plan. But his destiny quickly changes, and it seems that his mission fails when soldiers report him dead. When the family receives the news, they are devastated. It is the climax in the story's series of unfortunate events that ruin the Korean community's ability to sustain joy or hope during this historical period.

The war ends in 1945 when the US drops atomic bombs on Hiroshima and Nagasaki. The Japanese occupation of Korea also ends. Shockingly, Tae-yul arrives home from the war and explains how his mission failed but he had no way to contact his family since being jailed as a Japanese war prisoner. The story concludes by revealing that Abuji was secretly involved in Uncle's printing press, and Tae-yul—though confused by and angry about his country's plight—decides to re-open his Uncle's shop.

Chapters 1-5

Chapter 1 Summary: "Sun-hee (1940)"

Sun-hee, a young girl in a Korean family, is the novel's opening narrator. She is cleaning dishes in the kitchen while the nearby men in her family have a private conversation. They live in a Japanese-occupied country, and are under the imperialistic oversight of the Japanese government. Sun-hee's father (known simply as Abuji), her uncle, and her brother (Tae-yul) are discussing a rumor they heard about a new Japanese law taking effect, but Abuji doubts they will enact it (9). Sun-hee is secretly listening, though she is aware that it is not a young girl's place to partake in older men's business, so she pretends to be busy as they talk.

Sun-hee reveals that she is cunning and able to procure information from her uncle and older brother, but never asks her mother because it is useless to ask women about what the men know (11). Only men are allowed to have a voice, but Sun-hee has learned how to observe and ask questions in order to stay informed. Even though Sun-hee's father is a vice principal at the local school, he still is under the command of a Japanese principal and therefore has some level of status in the community but not as much as if he were Japanese. Everything taught at the school relates to Japanese history: "All our lessons were in Japanese. We studied Japanese language, culture, and history. Schools weren't allowed to teach Korean history or language" (12). Based on the tone of the male conversation, Sun-hee assumes things will change soon but not for the better.

Chapter 2 Summary: "Tae-yul"

Tae-yul is now the narrator. He explains how—since he's the first-born son—he's intimate with his father's thoughts. However, lately he senses confusion from his father and uncle and they haven't told him what is bothering them. Tae-yul is frustrated by this and also by his younger sister Sun-hee's constant questioning. One night, when uncle arrives to dinner early and furiously carries a newspaper, Tae-yul knows something is wrong. Uncle and Abuji argue in a separate room; when they emerge, they gather the family. They report that the Japanese government is "graciously" allowing Korean families to take a Japanese name in place of their Korean birth names, but it is a euphemism for declaring that the families must change their names (13). No one is happy. Their names carry meaning and tradition. Sun-hee, for example, means "great warmth" (13). Those who do not register with Japanese names will face arrest. While Uncle is furious, Abuji declares their new family name, "Kaneyama"—which secretly represents their Korean legacy of "mountains" and "gold" (15). They use a book of Japanese names to randomly select their first names. Tae-yul selects "Nobuo" (15).

Chapter 3 Summary: "Sun-hee"

Sun-hee has a flashback: four years ago, she and her family tuned into the Olympics. She remembers it fondly—the excitement and interest while cheering on the world's athletes. One night, they huddled around a radio together to listen to an Olympic race. But their mother, known only as "Omoni," had never finished school so couldn't understand the Japanese broadcaster. Instead, Uncle translates the event for her, interjecting goofy jokes and changing the narrative for entertainment. However, once the announcer declares the winner of the race as a Japanese participant (rather than by the runner's original Korean name and heritage), Uncle grows furious and knocks over the radio. Sun-hee is surprised and doesn't quite understand his anger, but her brother, Tae-yul, explains how it's shameful for Koreans to have their identity denied.

Chapter 4 Summary: "Tae-yul"

Tae-yul hasn't grown accustomed to his new name yet. He recalls how his Uncle reacted poorly to the Olympics incident. Angry after the marathon event, Uncle leaves and doesn't come back, so their father goes to find him. He eventually comes back with Uncle, who is savagely beat up. Uncle and his friends had gone out and crossed off the Japanese name of the athlete on local newspapers and replaced it with his Korean name. Japanese soldiers caught them, beat them up badly, and then threw them in jail. The Japanese later let a few of the men out—like Uncle—to send the community a warning. While Uncle recovers in the house, Tae-yul and Sun-hee keep him company. Uncle shows them the Korean flag by drawing it—an illegal act. The kids are amazed, since they have never seen their own country's flag during the Japanese occupation. Uncle makes them memorize it, then afterwards has them burn the drawing. He tells them both that a day will come when together they will raise the Korean flag on every rooftop. But Tae-yul wonders when that day will be.

Chapter 5 Summary: "Sun-hee"

When it's her turn, Sun-hee chooses the letter K in the Japanese name book. She changes her name to Keoko Kaneyama. The name translates to "girl" but also to the sun's "rays of brightness." She is happy when her father approves, aware of her name's multiple meanings (25). At school, the Korean students struggle to transition into calling their classmates and friends by new Japanese names. At first the teachers are tolerant, but they become increasingly strict with time. One day, when Sun-hee (Keoko) calls a classmate by their Korean name, the teacher (overseen by the Japanese military personnel at the school) punishes her. The teacher is hesitant, but with the soldier enforcing the rules, she lashes Sun-hee in front of the class. Sun-hee doesn't cry but gets angry. When she returns home, her mother is worried and applies medicinal herbs, but Sun-hee simply holds onto her anger.

At school, Sun-hee's best friend—Tomo, who's the son of the Japanese principal—struggles to call her by her new name, since he knows her as Sun-hee. They begin to joke about her Japanese name and make fun of it, which gives Sun-hee satisfaction: "I was also secretly pleased to be treating my Japanese name with such disrespect" (28). As time progresses, Sun-hee becomes interested in the Japanese alphabet, Kanji, which they learn in school. She is fascinated by the pictorial characters and how they can combine to make new words. She scores the highest in her class and receives an award for best Japanese speaker in her grade, but this brings negative attention as local boys begin to tease her and even throw rocks, calling her a "lover of Japan" (32). Saddened and alarmed, she begins to question herself; she doesn't support Japan though fears her proficiency with the language might suggest otherwise. When she gets home, her Uncle senses her sadness and teaches her that Kanji is actually an ancient language derived from Chinese culture, and that both Japanese and Koreans use it. This knowledge makes Sun-hee feel better about herself.

Chapters 1-5 Analysis

The narrative quickly fleshes out the world of a Korean family who is struggling with the loss of their heritage and forceable submission to Japanese imperialism. From the food they eat to the words they speak, authoritarian Japanese rulers suppress and regulate every aspect of their lives. Their dehumanization and stripping away of cultural pride is evident in how they must change their names, neglect their flag, and learn about another country's history while living on their own soil. The characterization of each family member begins to take shape differently within this context, as the ways in which each character resists change come up.

Abuji—the father—is rational and decisive, a community leader who remains calm and is able to subvert the oppressive conditions of the people to give secret meanings to his family's name and choices. For example, when Uncle is outraged by the legal name changes, Abuji strategically selects a name that clandestinely represents their Korean pride:

> [...] 'the Kim clan is a large and important one,' Abuji says. 'Long ago, all Kims lived in the same part of Korea, in the mountains. Choosing the word for gold as their name shows what a strong clan they were. Gold was only for kings.' He picks up the sheet of paper from the table and points at it. 'I have chosen our Japanese name. It will be Kaneyama. 'Yama' means 'mountain' in Japanese, and 'ka-ne' means 'gold.' So the name will honor our family history' (15).

His thoughtful choices and elusive resistance to Japanese occupation define him and his family, and create a foundation on which they can still be proud of their past. Abuji is calm, yet intelligent.

Uncle, on the other hand, represents a publicly aggressive and impetuous voice. He is proud of his Korean ancestry, but instead of being clever and subversive like Abuji, Uncle is bold and physical about his resistance. He and his friends receive a punishment for destroying the local newspapers: physical violence and incarceration. This reveals how the Japanese government is aggressive towards those who are outspoken, and how vocally expressing love for Korea can be a threat to the family's well-being. Uncle wants others to be aware of his struggle, and he embeds pride for Korea in the two young characters by showing them the flag. The symbolism of the flag is vibrant when Uncle draws it for the first time, but he then must burn it because of potential consequences. The erasure of Korean national memory is a forceful tactic used by the Japanese government to silence the hopes and imaginations of the people. The flag encapsulates the mythology of a nation, so by eliminating this aspect from Koreans, the Japanese are eliminating the myth and ethos of Koreans as well.

Schooling represents another tool in which the Japanese indoctrinate their ways into Korea's children. As a younger character, this is where Sun-hee must learn to fight her battles. In her Abuji and Uncle, Sun-hee has examples of how she can choose to reject Japanese imperialism: either by intellectual subversion or public resistance. Cleverly, she mixes both approaches. In school, she refuses to call others by their Japanese names and receives punishment from the teacher for it. But instead of submitting herself, she simply becomes angrier, and her anger fuels her detestation of Japanese ruling. She becomes more motivated and begins to master Kanji, the Japanese language, and becomes awarded with fluency in the complex linguistic system. This proves that she is intellectually capable of learning her oppressor's tongue. But later she learns that Kanji is rooted in ancient Chinese culture and that Koreans use it as well, revealing that perhaps the Japanese culture isn't as different from their own ancestors. This knowledge brings joy and pride to Sun-hee, who is still learning how to cope with the loss of her heritage.

It's clear that Sun-hee will continue to test boundaries and tamper with the rules until she is able to express herself. Unlike her brother, Tae-yul, and her mother—who is far less vocal or inquisitive—Sun-hee (Keoko) is looking for ways to understand her Korean identity under Japanese occupation. Sun-hee's boldness and intrepid courage—despite being the youngest family member and daughter—are defining marks of her character at this point in the narrative, perhaps a foreshadow to her role in the story's outcome.

Chapters 6-9

Chapter 6 Summary: "Tae-yul (1941)"

Tae-yul and Sun-hee are studying kanji, but Tae-yul is visibly frustrated. He is an average student and not interested in his academics, even though his father and grandpa were high-achieving scholars. He expresses his discontent with studying kanji, and Sun-hee—who is more advanced even at a younger age—tries to help him. She explains how she assigns each pictorial character a story, and that helps her remember and enjoy each word. Tae-yul scoffs at her, and Sun-hee seems hurt that he is dismissive. Tae-yul prefers to work on motor scooters with his Uncle, and he excels at it. But he feels guilty since his father is the vice principal and seemingly has high expectations for him at school. Tae-yul is excited when one evening his Uncle calls him over to help finish working on a scooter together.

Chapter 7 Summary: "Sun-hee"

The war in Europe has started as a result of the rise of Hitler's Nazis. Sun-hee isn't interested in that war because there is another war closer to home—between Japan and Manchuria. The Japanese soldiers are occupying Korea because it allows easier access to controlling the region, and the troops often require the local rice supplies. Sun-hee doesn't like this, just as she doesn't like how Tae-yul can ride bicycles but she can't because she's a girl. Instead she must help Omoni cook dinner, but the rice supply is low. Even the barley substitute is running dry, so Omoni uses chicken feed as dinner. Sun-hee can't believe it, but Omoni assures her it is nutritious. Sun-hee thinks to herself, "I could hardly believe we were cooking animal food for our dinner" (42). No one seems to enjoy the meal but they respectfully eat it in silence.

The Japanese government passes another law, this time declaring certain Korean trees illegal, and enforcing the Japanese Cherry Blossom as the only tree Koreans can plant. Omoni recruits her children to help uproot her garden's "rose of Sharon trees" (45), but decides to illegally keep one of them in a large vase. Sun-hee is both scared and proud that her mother chose to do this. Later, the Japanese soldiers patrol the neighborhood to oversee the burning of the community's rose of Sharon trees. They approve of Sun-hee's family's work and don't find the hidden tree. Sun-hee admits that the Cherry Blossoms are more beautiful, but that she can't wait to see when the rose of Sharon trees will be blooming in Korean once again.

Chapter 8 Summary: "Tae-yul"

Tae-yul is helping Uncle in his print shop, and now that he is older and able to arrive on his bicycle, Uncle lets him stay and help longer. His Uncle is a printshop maker, but his business is beginning to slow down due to the Japanese occupation and war. To help his business stay afloat, he decides to provide his services to not only Korean customers, but Japanese merchants as well, since they have "deeper pockets" (50). Abuji is concerned, and Tae-yul does not approve, but Uncle goes ahead and starts to befriend the Japanese, treating them with better service than he did his Korean customers. This new business move increases tension in the house between Abuji and Uncle. As the older brother, Abuji does not approve and expresses disagreement. Uncle has no option, however, and tells Abuji that he can leave the house in order to continue his new business. While Abuji and Uncle argue, Tae-yul and Sun-hee are secretly listening from outside, and they both want to help. They agree to think of a plan together, but Tae-yul is only doing it to get Sun-hee off his back. He worries about his Uncle becoming a "chin-il-pa" (Japanese lover) and fears that patriotic Koreans who disapprove of his actions might hurt or even kill Uncle (53).

Chapter 9 Summary: "Sun-hee"

Sun-hee spends time with her friend, Pak sung-joon, and together they enjoy whatever small treats they can afford. Sun-hee wants to take her to Uncle's shop, partly so she can investigate what her Uncle is up to. When she takes her friend, Uncle is as friendly as always, but his demeanor changes when Pak sung-joon explains that her family is new to town and her dad works at the local bank. Sun-hee notices her Uncle's change of expression. Uncle further confuses her when he suddenly tells them that he's busy and escorts them out. He seems vigilant and Sun-hee is surprised, since it is unusual for her Uncle—who is typically jovial and enthusiastic. When she returns home, she decides not to tell Tae-yul about her observations, and they continue planning on how to help the family.

When the news breaks out about Pearl Harbor, Tae-yul rushes home excitedly and has his family turn on the radio. They listen together. Abuji is concerned that hard times will follow. Uncle soon arrives, also in excitement, and asks if Tae-yul can miss school to help him print flyers about the war at the request of a Japanese administrator. Abuji hesitantly agrees, and Tae-yul runs off with Uncle. Sun-hee is jealous that she can't be involved, so takes a walk nearby and runs into her old friend, Tomo. He is outside with his male friends, and they are playing with Tomo's new war plane model. Tomo allows Sun-hee to hold it, even though he doesn't let his friends touch it. The boys become animated and start chanting "Kill the Americans!" (62). Tomo joins in and leads their growing excitement. Sun-hee remembers a movie that they had to watch in school—the first film she has ever seen—about Japanese war propaganda explaining how the Americans would kill anyone with "black hair" (63). The boys use the film to justify their hatred of America. Sun-hee becomes alarmed at how the boys are so eager for war and killing, and she walks off.

Chapters 6-9 Analysis

Divisions and rivalries fill the narrative, and they continue to grow: Japanese culture versus Korean customs, male privilege versus female responsibility, the law versus morality, and the Axis versus Allies are a few prominent themes to note. The gap between how the Japanese are enforcing their rules of living onto the Koreans—making them uproot their trees and burn them, for example—increases in this chapter, and the complexity of the situation begins to reveal other areas of inequality within the family unit. For instance, the distance between Sun-hee and her brother, Tae-yul, becomes more pronounced. Tae-yul is more trained to be a manual laborer, whereas Sun-hee seems destined for an intellectual direction. Though Sun-hee feels just as capable of doing physical work, she does not receive the same opportunities as her brother—Uncle asks Tae-yul to help with physical tasks. This gender gap is one of the tensions in the household, but not the only one.

In another moment of discrepancy, Sun-hee feels torn about her mother, who technically breaks the law by keeping a rose of Sharon tree. Sun-hee feels conflicted, because she understands her mother's pride in wanting to keep Korea's national tree, but also knows that the new Japanese law forbids it. It forces her to confront her beliefs and morals like never before, where she must decide whether it is ever acceptable to disregard a rule if that rule is inherently biased and hateful. She decides that she is proud of her mom, but still fears that there may be future consequences:

> Omoni was breaking the law. If she got caught—if the guards discovered the little tree—what would happen? Would she be arrested? A cold wind blew through me. I was afraid for her. But I was proud of her, too. How could I be proud of my mother for breaking the law? I shook my head, trying to clear it of these confusing thoughts, and looked at Omoni again (45).

The symbolism of this moment is powerful—a mother preserving the roots of an outlawed tree, while her daughter observes the act of love. It serves as one of a few instances in the novel where characters must reconfigure their sense of right and wrong, since the usual rules are less applicable during wartime.

Sun-hee is not the only character struggling to understand her feelings during the Japanese occupation; Uncle also feels pressured to make changes to his ideology and actions. Due to slow business, his choice to collaborate with Japanese merchants complicates his identity as a Korean, since he is "selling out" to the enemy. His decision allows his business to stay open during tough times, but it also creates friction and disagreement in the house, where Abuji worries of the effects on his family's reputation. Knowing that a "chin-il-pa" (53), or Japanese lover, can draw negative attention, Uncle has no choice but to risk his own and his family's safety in order to keep his printing press open. This hard choice once again emphasizes the difficult choices families must make in times of war, and how even someone like Uncle—who is a vocal and brash Korean loyalist—has to sacrifice his beliefs.

The characters who don't seem as affected in this story are the young men, who have the privilege of youthful innocence, male excitement, and interest in warfare. This gung-ho attitude appears in both Tae-yul and Tomo. The war captivates Tae-yul, and his lack of concern about the repercussions of entering war with the United States shows how jubilant he is when hearing the news of invasion. Rather than being worried, his role of importance increases when Uncle asks him to help print flyers about the war, and his emphasis on boring school work further decreases. Similarly, Tomo—who is Japanese and therefore has reason to be supportive of the war—is equally excited, best illustrated in the scene where he plays with his war planes and his friends chant "Kill the Americans!" (62). Their sense of propaganda-infused war support is palpable, yet whereas Sun-hee is against the idea of killing, the boys are naively in favor of battle.

Chapters 10-14

Chapter 10 Summary: "Tae-yul (1942)"

Tae-yul is riding home on his bike when he sees a plane flying overhead for the first time. He is in awe and accidentally falls over since he has never seen a plane before. As the war progresses, Japan continues to conquer new territories, and the students learn about it all in school. Tae-yul feels conflicted by the Japanese dominance because he knows it complicates life for Koreans, who benefit but also suffer from Japanese occupation. Tae-yul imagines what it would be like to fly a plane, and fantasizes about the thrill of being a pilot.

Chapter 11 Summary: "Sun-hee"

With the escalation of the war, the Japanese army has become stricter in Korea. They introduce a system for residential gatherings in case of a war emergency, and the neighbors must practice how to organize themselves for military roll calls. During a practice session, the soldiers appear and begin to yell at everyone to get in line outside of their house and count off. Sun-hee describes a neighbor who is an old widow, shunned and neglected by the community because it views her as "bad luck" (68). She lives by herself and doesn't speak Japanese, so when the soldier gets to her, she is unable to call out her number in Japanese and says "six" in Korean instead (70). The soldier beats her in front of everyone, saying she has a brain of "dung" for not being able to speak Japanese (70). Once he moves on, Omoni tries to help her up, but the soldier gets angry. Omoni explains that she is an elder and needs assistance.

Her mother's courage stuns Sun-hee, and the soldier surprisingly allows them to take the old widow inside her home. Sun-hee feels guilty because she could have helped the widow by telling her the Japanese word for six while standing in line, but instead she had just mumbled it to herself out of fear of the soldiers. If she had used her voice—like her mother—she might have prevented the beating. To make up for it, she stays at the widow's house to teach her how to count in Japanese. However, after only teaching her five numbers, the old woman says she refuses to learn more because she will not allow the Japanese to own her "thoughts" (73). Knowing this, Sun-hee tells Omoni, and Omoni makes Sun-hee promise that she will help the widow to be the first outside during a roll call. Sun-hee is hesitant, but agrees.

Chapter 12 Summary: "Tae-yul (1942-1943)"

Tae-yul finds the "neighborhood accountings" to be "such a nuisance" (74). He hides in the house while the countdown takes place, but Omoni grows worried that the soldiers will find out so he never does it again. During school, the students receive rubber balls from the Japanese Emperor in honor of Japan's victories in tropical islands with large rubber production. The children begin to play with their balls but the school's military personnel suddenly stop them and make them recite their gratitude for the Emperor's generosity. This ruins Tae-yul's mood, who rationalizes:

> But I don't feel like playing anymore—all because of that stupid announcement. 'Express your gratitude,' they'd said. What they take: our rice, our language,

our names. What they give: little rubber balls. I can't feel grateful about such a bad deal (76).

Tae-yul then refuses to play with his friends that day.

The accountings continue to increase. Tae-yul explains his dislike for how the residents must praise the "Imperial Army" and must also offer their supplies to soldiers if needed (76). He and Uncle are angry, but Abuji tells them there is no use for anger. Tae-yul questions how his father is not angrier. During winter, the soldiers take jackets and blankets from families, and Tae-yul's discontent continues to grow. One afternoon, Tae-yul is riding his bike home when two soldiers shout for him to stop. They probe him and the bicycle. Tae-yul feels uncomfortable. Abuji comes outside and the soldiers address him as "sensei" (77)—the teacher—informing him that they will need to take Tae-yul's bike for the Imperial Army. When they try to confiscate it, Tae-yul resists, but Abuji only apologizes to the soldiers and they take it from him. As they walk away, they laugh and make jokes. Tae-yul, infuriated, criticizes his dad's response. Abuji walks away and apologizes to his son, but Tae-yul believes Abuji doesn't care.

Chapter 13 Summary: "Sun-hee"

Sun-hee senses anger and sadness from Tae-yul but doesn't know why. She sees him walking to school the next morning instead of riding his bike like usual, but she hasn't heard anything about the bike incident so can only make guesses. At home, Tae-yul and Abuji are tense, and Sun-hee grows uncomfortable. To make matters worse, Uncle isn't around as often because he works longer hours at his shop. When Sun-hee brings him dinner one night, and notices he is acting strangely. One night, when she is going to take him food, she receives an unexpectedly visit from her old friend, Tomo, who is hiding in the shadows.

His visit is a surprise, and Sun-hee is confused since they no longer attend school together. He talks about their childhood and is acting strangely, making comments about her Uncle and how nice he was to them. When he leaves, Sun-hee thinks that he might've been sending a message to warn her about Uncle. She runs to his shop—careful that Japanese patrollers don't intercept her—and frantically explains herself. Uncle seems prepared, and begins to pack his materials. He thanks her for being "very brave" (86), and tells her to ask Tae-yul for more details. He says he will be leaving for an indefinite amount of time. Sun-hee feels scared but proud that she helped warn him.

Chapter 14 Summary: "Tae-yul"

Sun-hee returns home to inform the family about Uncle's departure. Abuji is concerned and simply says they will tell others they don't know where he went. Abuji also warns the family that no one can leave the house that night. Sun-hee exits the room looking frightened, so Tae-yul goes after her. She tells him that Uncle gave her permission to know more, so Tae-yul explains what he has recently learned. Uncle secretly works for a Korean resistance group and has been printing newsletters at night. His partnership with the Japanese was a front to seem like a "chin-il-pa" (Japanese lover) so that he could avoid Imperial scrutiny (87). Sun-hee tells Tae-yul that Tomo warned her and she informed Uncle, and Tae-yul is surprised by this news. Their parents only know that Uncle is in the resistance, but nothing else.

Tae-yul tells his sister that he is grateful for their Uncle, who has kept him informed while Abuji "buries himself in his books" (89). Tae-yul is critical of his father; he doesn't believe his father cares about what happens to Koreans. Sun-hee defends Abuji by saying it's his role to keep everyone safe. Tae-yul counters by saying that Uncle is the real hero: "what Uncle and others like him are doing—it's more important than anything. We aren't Japanese—we're Korean. But we'll never be allowed to truly be Korean unless we have our independence" (90). Sun-hee continues to push back, asking if that's more important than family allegiance. Tae-yul explains that without a rebellion from men like Uncle, there will be no Korean families left to defend.

They agree to keep everything a secret and return inside and pretend to study. Then, a neighborhood accounting takes place in the night. They scramble to get the widow and organize themselves—since accountings only happen in the day—and worry that it might be about Uncle. Instead, the leader demands that every family collect the metals in their household and offer it to the Imperial Army's "divine" mission (92). The family gathers their jewelry, family heirlooms, tools, and other metal objects. Sun-hee begs her mother not to get rid of a golden dragon brooch that was a gift. Omoni thinks about it, then hides it in her underwear. The family is tense, but all agree, and give the rest to the soldiers. The chapter ends when Tae-yul decides to sneak out to see Uncle's shop, but everything seems normal there. He worries that Sun-hee made a mistake, and runs home to let her know.

Chapters 10-14 Analysis

Ownership and resistance continue to develop as major threads in the narrative as different characters express their feelings about losing their heritage. Secrets (like Uncle's involvement in the Korean rebellion movement) and personal loss (like soldiers taking Tae-yul's bike) continue to mount and begin to test the relationships of family, friends, and community in times of war. The growing sense of military control is evident as Japanese soldiers begin to have daily "neighborhood accountings" in which they essentially raid the privacy of each Korean family.

In Chapter 11, it reaches a climax when Sun-hee's widowed neighbor—an old woman who lives alone and can't speak Japanese—receives a beating from an intolerant soldier. In the aftermath, Sun-hee's attempt to help the woman snags when the old woman surprisingly refuses to learn how to count numbers in Japanese—an act that she must do for the neighborhood roll calls. When Sun-hee asks, the widow simply says, "They cannot have my thoughts. I will not allow it" (73). This is a pivotal and symbolic moment in the text, when an elder reveals that she refuses to give the Japanese Imperial Army more than her body. At this point, the Japanese occupation has taken the body, the tongue (language), and even the heritage (names) of the Korean population; however, in this moment, a small resistance happens against losing the mind and spirit.

Furthermore, this section fleshes out how community operates during this time. Sun-hee, a young girl who would typically avoid interacting with the widow since the woman is "bad luck" is now in a position to help her neighbor, and that is what she chooses to do. In these moments, love, trust, and resistance begin to form away from the invasive oversight of the soldiers, and it's where Sun-hee is able to develop her sense of self during the war.

Meanwhile, as Sun-hee strengthens her role of support with the community, Tae-yul's frustration and anger continue to rise and push him away from others, including his own father. After losing his bicycle to Japanese soldiers in

Chapter 12—who claim they need it for the army but seem more like disrespectful and untrustworthy bullies abusing their power—it's clear that Tae-yul strongly dislikes the suppression of Korean freedom. The loss of his material object exemplifies his biggest possession stolen at the hands of Japanese imperialism. He struggles to understand why his father and other Koreans tolerate such an erasure of their Korean pride. It begins to fracture his sense of self and his understanding of the world, best highlighted in how he begins to question and disrespect his father, whom Tae-yul believes "doesn't care" about what's happening and is irresponsibly "burying himself in his books" (79). Uncle's stance as a secret member of the Korean rebellion begins to appeal more to Tae-yul, who sees there are two ways for men to respond to their national crisis: by acquiescing (like his father) or by organizing a resistance (like Uncle).

All of these events of discomfort, invasion, and imperial abuse erode at the cores of each character, and they all find different ways to cope. Despite their efforts, there is a visible deterioration of traditional values (family, culture, respect, friends, etc.) as they must all reconfigure their set of beliefs and learn who they can trust, since fear and death is an immediate presence. For example, friends like Tomo, who alerted Sun-hee about Uncle's danger, start to raise questions rather than gratitude. This confusion and conflict of morals and allegiance appears in the argument between Sun-hee and Tae-yul, when the older brother tries to convince his sister of his views:

> 'What Uncle and others like him are doing—it's more important than anything. We aren't Japanese—we're Korean. But we'll never be allowed to truly be Korean unless we have our independence.' 'More important than family?' she asks. But it's not one of her usual whiny little-sister questions. She's thinking

hard, I can tell. 'Our duty to Abuji is important,' I
say. 'It's a part of our culture. But if the Japanese
have their way, someday there won't be any such
thing as our culture. When Uncle works for
independence, he works for the right to live as Abuji
wants us to...Do you see what I mean?' [...] It's so
confusing. Uncle acting like chin-il-pa when he's not.
Tomo, the son of an important Japanese official,
helping a resistance worker...Uncle disobeying Abuji
in order to be able to obey him one day. If I can't
fully understand, how can she? (90).

During war, there is no sense of normalcy and each
character must scramble to determine where they stand in
an ever-shifting landscape of fear and betrayal. Tae-yul
grows further apart from his father, Uncle is on the run, and
Sun-hee is torn between loyalty to her parents' culture or
joining her brother in revolutionizing her views.

Chapters 15-20

Chapter 15 Summary: "Sun-hee"

Tae-yul is angry at Sun-hee. He shouts and grabs her by the
arm. He is upset that Sun-hee informed Uncle to leave,
since Tae-yul believes Uncle was not in danger. Sun-hee
begins to think that Tomo was warning her about the metal
and not about Uncle. Abuji intervenes but Tae-yul is
furious, which causes Sun-hee to cry. Abuji tries to comfort
her by explaining that the Japanese would have inevitably
discovered and imprisoned Uncle, and that warning him
was the right thing to do. Tae-yul disagrees. Tae-yul and
Uncle have shared their bedroom since Sun-hee was born,
which explains why Tae-yul feels so connected to him.
Sun-hee goes to the bedroom she shares with her parents
and cries. She feels guilty, and Omoni tries to console her,

but she feels even worse. She admits she wanted to feel like a hero and save Uncle rather than thinking through the risks.

Chapter 16 Summary: "Tae-yul"

A "neighborhood accounting" escalates when soldiers announce there is "a traitor" and conduct a house-to-house search. They are looking for Uncle, whose shop they have raided and who they have declared as a "criminal" (99). Looking for information, the soldiers take Abuji into the police station for further questioning. The family is fearful but can do nothing. After many hours, he comes home late but unscathed. Tae-yul—who was extremely concerned about soldiers taking his father—knows that Uncle was smart for not sharing his secrets with the family because it kept them safe.

As time passes, soldiers closely watch the family by keeping an eye on their house. But over time, Tae-yul tries to live normally, and even forgives his sister. The war is taking up more time and resources, and students must now gather pine roots from the forest so that the soldiers can use them as grease, since oil and other supplies are dwindling. Tae-yul has splinters in his hands daily and his mom must treat his hands every night. When the Japanese government announces they will be building an airstrip near the city and asks for volunteers, Tae-yul signs up, eager to get out of school and apply his technical craft elsewhere. Abuji does not approve, but Tae-yul respectfully points out how his schooling has only turned into war propaganda, so Abuji allows him to work on the airfield. After weeks of grueling work and abusive manual labor, he earns his "Japanese Youth Air Corps" badge for his contributions (105). He tells the family he will have access to the planes for cleaning, and that he might even be able to sit in the pilot seat one day.

Chapter 17 Summary: "Sun-hee (1943–44)"

Without a radio, the family does not have access to information, but it's clear that Japan is losing the war. At school, students spend all their time helping the war effort—filling sandbags, sharpening bamboo sticks for weapons, gathering rocks to throw at enemies in case of invasion, and even learning how to lethally bayonet a soldier. Sun-hee strangely enjoys the work because it exhausts her and takes her mind off worries, but she laughs at how ridiculous the idea of defending Japanese imperialism against US aid would be. One afternoon at school, a plane flies overhead; it is not the usual drill. Students panic, some cry, but Sun-hee is aware and alert.

The plane drops leaflets instead of bombs. Japanese soldiers announce that they must retrieve and burn all leaflets. Sun-hee secretly keeps one. When she gets home she shows Tae-yul, who also has a leaflet he kept. They ask Abuji to read it because it's written in Korean, and only the elders can read Korean since Japan has occupied their country for so long. Abuji reads it to himself and burns it, then tells his children it's from US Army General MacArthur, saying: "it is known that the Korean people are not America's enemies, and he promises that Korea will never be bombed by American planes" (111). This brings Sun-hee joy; she is ecstatic the US distinguishes Koreans from Japanese.

She begins to think about what makes Koreans different, since she reads, writes, and communicates within Japanese society. She realizes Korea is her Uncle drawing the flag; her mother who kept the rose of Sharon tree; and the next door widow who refused to learn Japanese numbers. They all have found ways to resist Japanese imperialism. Since Sun-hee's private thoughts are always in Korean, she also shows resistance to Japanese occupation and is therefore Korean. Sun-hee asks Abuji to teach her Hangul—the ancient Korean language. He promises one day but not while soldiers watch them so closely (due to the risks). She writes in her diary instead to collect her thoughts.

War efforts increase, and older girls at school must leave home and work for the Japanese army abroad. Few girls volunteer, so many face random selection. Soldiers choose one girl but she is instantly sent back, and Sun-hee knows it's because her family must be "chin-il-pa" (116). The girl is Sun-hee's best friend's sister, and Sun-hee begins to question if she can be friends with her anymore, since her family might secretly be Japanese supporters.

Chapter 18 Summary: "Tae-yul"

Sun-hee tells her brother about her suspicions of Jung-shin's family. He admits they must be chin-il-pa and advises Sun-hee to be careful of what she says around her friend. That night, soldiers burst into their home and order everyone to stand outside in the cold. They search the house for "treasonous writings" (121). Tae-yul notices Sun-hee seems worried. The captain goes through the papers retrieved by soldiers. Sun-hee's diary is there. She surprises Tae-yul when she becomes bold and claims it as hers. After reading it, the captain gives her a warning and has it burned.

The event reminds him of a story Uncle had shared with him, about how their grandfather worked hard to become a scholar. He received a jade button to wear after studying his whole life. Shortly after, the Japanese occupation began and the Japanese soldiers demanded he remove the button and cut his top-knot hair—Korean marks of a scholar. He refused. Soldiers came into their home and forcefully cut the man's hair, stole his jade symbol, and then threw his hair into the kimchee pot. Shortly after, Tae-yul's grandfather died. Tae-yul feels angry and incapacitated. For the first time, he understands why his father does not defend his family; there is nothing a Korean citizen can do against the tyranny of Japanese imperialism.

Chapter 19 Summary: "Sun-hee"

Sun-hee is sad about her diary. She was keeping it to give Uncle upon his return. Abuji tells her he is proud of her and that "they burn the paper, not the words" (125). Inspired, she begins a new diary, feeling proud and re-energized to express herself. She realizes how important Korean language, history, culture, and customs are to her and she cannot wait to learn more about her heritage as soon as Japan loses the war.

Chapter 20 Summary: "Tae-yul"

Tae-yul learns about kamikaze pilots—suicide bombers in the Japanese air fleet. He is interested and impressed by their feats and befriends a regular patrolmen—whom he refers to as "space face" (129)—to learn more about the kamikaze. The soldiers regales Te-yul with stories of their glory and heroism. Tae-yul admires kamikazes and imagines being one.

Chapters 15-20 Analysis

Though extremely important, Park does not mention the setting very often. There are references to national plants, gardens, and trees that are common in Korea, but besides the location and historical time period of the book, there isn't much reference to the land. Yet, when it appears, it often carries meaning, and represents the state of the nation's internal condition. A rare description of the surrounding terrain reveals:

> Our town was surrounded by mountains. Before the war those mountains had been covered with forests. When the Japanese took all the coal and oil for the war effort, we had to use wood for fuel. One after another, trees were chopped down, until at last there was hardly a tree anywhere. We used to be able to see green and pleasant slopes. Now they were brown, gray, dead (115).

The connotation of this loss, desolation, and hopelessness underscores the reality for Koreans.

With war taking hold, conflict in the family increases, and new strains appear both in the family and their community. They suffer their first major loss when Uncle has to flee due to the dangerous climate. This moment is a crucial element in the story's rising action, which indicates that tensions are escalating and building towards a climax and resolution. Uncle's departure is the biggest challenge for the family thus far, and since they are a close-knit family and unsure how to deal with his absence, it creates a rift. A sense of guilt and loss begins to emerge, especially for Sun-hee, who blames herself after Tae-yul accuses her of making a grave mistake.

An underlying theme in this gravitational moment is the weight of gender expectations, since Tae-yul believes his foolish young sister didn't have the right to inform Uncle without first consulting him, the elder brother. Sun-hee's character is bold, decisive, and fearless, but as a young

Korean girl, these are attributes that seem to keep working against her. Unlike her brother—whose involvement in the "Japanese Youth Air Corps" indicates a rising interest in war activity—Sun-hee does not have an outlet to express her boldness. So she turns to her diary and begins to voice her anger, fear, and frustration in a way that is socially acceptable and secretive for a young Korean girl. This suppression of her character is perhaps representative of a larger suppression, layered with war, family, gender expectations, generational family norms, and cultural customs. Sun-hee, more than any other character, receives the brunt of all this. It's no surprise then, that she must turn to small acts of rebellion to validate her own identity.

When soldiers burn her diary, the act magnifies how much loss she—and her people—must endure. The destroyed diary is, in symbolic fashion, the attempt to destroy her innermost privacy, her sense of self and comfort, and her Korean voice. Even though it endangers her family, she refuses this silence and begins to write again, evincing her character's deep sense of justice, freedom, and pride. Her cultural and political awareness grows from her oppression, and she begins to understand the power of her language and voice: "But it was important. Our stories, our names, our alphabet. Even Uncle's newspaper. It was all about words. If words weren't important, they wouldn't try so hard to take them away" (127). More than any other character, Sun-hee is growing into herself, her community, and her power, and doing so through her passion for Korean identity and language.

But her lost diary isn't the only form of inhumanity and destruction experienced during this section of the novel. The motif of Japanese abuse appears again and again, in various parts of characters' memories. For Abuji and Uncle, they have witnessed it as children, when soldiers disrespected their father in his home. The scene of his "scholarly" ponytail as it is cut and then thrown into the kimchee pot is horrific imagery of how invasive and cruel the Japanese occupation is (124). The elderly father dies one month after, due to a "broken heart," which suggests that Japanese imperialism causes more than psychological trauma—it literally consumes innocent Korean lives (125).

Each character must deal with this cruelty and abuse, yet they must also find ways to overcome with resilience, hope, and dreams of a brighter future. Though rare, these moments appear in these chapters in small ways. For Tae-yul, he seems to find it in his circumvention of the Japanese education system, electing to leave the classroom in order to work on the air strip outside of town. His enthusiasm and interest reignites his joy, as he is no longer learning about useless war propaganda but is instead applying his skills as a young man in a manual trade. There are undertones of his desire to become a pilot, even a "kamikaze," and it gives him a new purpose. For Abuji, he must learn how to console his household in times of despair, and to provide guidance in darkness.

In the scene when American airplanes drop pamphlets into the streets—which the Japanese army forbids people taking home—the children disobey the law and bring it to Abuji. Instead of scolding them, he is able to translate the text since no one else can read Korean like him, and he shares the information before burning it. This reveals that Abuji, like other characters, is also able to resist Japanese occupation, just in smaller and less obvious ways. The message he reads brings hope to the children, who find comfort in the solidarity of American soldiers. Interestingly, this is a turning point in the tone of the story, when everyone, particularly Sun-hee, begin to regain a sense of Korea's beauty:

What did it mean to be Korean, when for all my life Korea had been part of Japan? It took the words of a man I'd never heard of—a faraway American—to make me realize something that had been inside me all along. Korean was the jokes and stories Uncle told us. It was the flag he'd drawn. It was the rose of Sharon tree Omoni had saved, and the little circle Tae-yul had carved on the bottom of the gourd bowls. Korean was the thoughts of Mrs. Ahn, in her own language, not someone else's (111).

The message from US Army General MacArthur helps everyone perceive hope more clearly and optimistically. Even Tae-yul begins to understand his father's clandestine and quiet resistance more open-heartedly. At this point, the mood of the narrative begins to introduce hints of happiness and confidence in understanding how to fight against Japanese imperialism. In the words of Sun-hee, "You burn the paper but not the words. You silence the words but not the thoughts. You kill the thoughts only if you kill the man. And you will find that his thoughts rise again in the minds of others—twice as strong as before!" (126).

Chapters 21-25

Chapter 21 Summary: "Sun-hee (1945)"

Sun-hee still hasn't spoken to her friend, Jung-shin, after learning she is "chin-il-pa." Jung-shin has seemed distressed and distant. But one day Sun-hee sees her walking in town and begins to joke with her. Jung-shin lights up, and they rekindle their friendship. Sun-hee is glad she is regaining some semblance of normal life. But later, at dinner, Tae-yul asks to speak privately with Abuji. The women leave to wash the dishes, but they can hear the argument. When they finally return, Tae-yul announces that he has enlisted in the Japanese Imperial Army, distressing, saddening, and angering his family. Tae-yul tries to explain himself, saying that if he joins, the army will provide better supplies for the family and they will benefit from his sacrifice. Omoni disagrees and worries about his death. Sun-hee feels overwhelmed by the cruel effects of the Japanese occupation and runs out. Tae-yul goes after her and tells her he has a secret: Uncle is alive and working for the resistance.

Chapter 22 Summary: "Tae-yul"

One day after enlisting, Tae-yul goes to the police station to talk to an officer. He is nervous, and when he arrives, they interrogate him about his uncle. An officer wants Tae-yul to bring his uncle in to be "reeducated" (140) and join the Japanese. Tae-yul listens, and suppresses his laughter at the ludicrous idea of Uncle supporting the Japanese. Tae-yul stays "one step ahead" of predicting the officer's intentions (142). He "acts" like he cares and tells the officer he cannot help because he is joining the military and doesn't know where his uncle is (143). The officer is disappointed, but congratulates him. Tae-yul is willing to do whatever it takes to assist his uncle, even risking his own life.

Chapter 23 Summary: "Sun-hee"

The night before leaving, Tae-yul meets with Sun-hee and tells her that Uncle is alive and represents a threat to the Japanese police, which is a sign that he is succeeding. They are both proud of Uncle. But Sun-hee is sad and ashamed she cannot be more helpful to her brother. Tae-yul says he will be able to write letters, though the Japanese will censor them. Sun-hee should be extra aware of any coded meanings he might be trying to communicate while training

33

with the army. They make jokes about Tae-yul's poor handwriting and embrace before he leaves the next day. Sun-hee tries to write in her journal about it, but she is unable to articulate her feelings, filled with too much pain and loss in Uncle's and now her brother's departure.

Chapter 24 Summary: "Tae-yul"

Tae-yul is on the train to Seoul. He keeps his belongings close as reminders of home. He opens a gift from Sun-hee: a dried petal wrapped in paper. It's a rose of Sharon, Korea's national flower. Tae-yul knows it might raise alarm during inspection, so he crushes it, but will remember it. In boot camp, he learns how to perform the basic functions of a soldier. It is a grueling experience as a recruit. Besides having to memorize the Emperor's speeches, the commanding officers physically abuse the men, often whipping, clubbing, or hitting them for the smallest mistakes. The soldiers tell the recruits that they are being prepared to withstand pain from the enemy. A few recruits don't last and return home in disgrace. But not Tae-yul, who is determined to make his Uncle and family proud.

Chapter 25 Summary: "Sun-hee"

Abuji is thrilled when the family receives their first letter from Tae-yul. They read it together. Tae-yul sounds happy, though exhausted. Sun-hee asks to borrow the letter and spends her morning deciphering it. His writing alludes to how the Japanese army is struggling to supply new recruits, and Sun-hee determines that Tae-yul is letting her know that the Japanese army is losing more battles than winning. This is good news, since it means the war could end soon. The family makes a care package to send him. They each write letters—Sun-hee helps Omoni write hers—and deliver the care package with snacks and treats. Omoni asks the next door widow, Mrs. Ahn, if she can spare persimmons from her tree. Every year, the Japanese soldiers come and take the fruit from her tree, but Mrs. Ahn manages to secretly keep some. She gives the family everything she has left, which Sun-hee is grateful for, but wishes she had more for herself. They send it all to Tae-yul because it is his favorite snack. Sun-hee's spirits are high.

Chapters 21-25 Analysis

Despite the ever-present onus of war, the family continues to generate hope. Old friendships endure, characters make bold decisions, and Tae-yul's plan to join the army—once seen as reckless—begins to yield benefits. The characters are learning how to deal with loss, and are even able to transform their pain into power. For example, when Tae-yul must crush the flower that Sun-hee gives him, he simply blows the ashes and promises to remember her intentions. It displays that physical objects may be restricted by the Japanese, but the emotional and spiritual value of them does not diminish: "I crumble the flower in my fist. Then I open my hand and blow the little pink pieces away. It's OK, Sun-hee, I say to myself. I don't need the flower. I'll remember without it" (149). This transcendence of the material world is a sign of Tae-yul's growth and ability to grasp the symbolic weight of Sun-hee's subversive intentions.

However, there are still instances of pain and suffering. Omoni—a quiet character in both voice and physical presence—struggles with her son leaving for war. Abuji—a typically calm and practical man—yells and becomes angry for the first time. Sun-hee—a deeply thoughtful young girl—cannot comprehend the amount of abuse perpetrated by the Japanese. Perhaps the cruelest scene is when soldiers strip Abuji's father of his hard-earned scholarly titles and treat him like a dog in his own house. The complete lack of agency in moments like these are lessons to Tae-yul about how dehumanizing and belittling Koreans feel, and how powerless each individual actually is.

His anger builds, but he is able to harness it to empower himself and his community, as he grows determined to fight back: "They're doing it again. Taking whatever they want. Grandfather's hair, Omoni's jewelry, Sun-hee's diary. My bicycle. And we can't do anything to stop them. Now it's Uncle they want. And they want me to stand there and do nothing again. This time, I have to do something" (141). His family's legacy of loss goes from a painful history into a hopeful future, as he galvanizes himself to action by joining the military. The novel largely documents how humans must constantly evolve and shift their morals, beliefs, and ways of being in order to endure tragic history—even it if means risking one's life. Their understanding of themselves as individuals—but also as community members, as friends, as role models, as men and women—changes as often as new information about the war arises.

The bootcamp shows how physically brutal—and downright desperate—Japanese imperialism has become. Tae-yul witnesses and tolerates abuse as a soldier recruit in order to increase his family's chances of comfort and survival. It's a strange territory for anyone to be in: serving the country that imprisons you, but doing so out of love for your real country's honor. The concept of "acting" appears in these chapters, as Tae-yul begins to understand that his external image may not necessarily reflect his true intentions, and he begins to play this game of pretending to advance his and his family's situation.

However, it comes at a psychological price, as he must code every decision and trust that Sun-hee will be able to decipher his message: "I'll be allowed to write letters, but I'm sure they'll be censored. I won't be able to put down the truth as I see it. I'm counting on you to read between my words and uncover their true meaning" (144). The heightened sense of codes, secrecy, and clandestine efforts are a reminder of the many shapes and forms that resistance can take. In this case, Tae-yul leverages his sister's intelligence to use her as a tool for communication in an otherwise "censored" arena. It largely represents the dual lives of Koreans having to adopt two personalities and two existences just to maintain their one purpose of maintaining a respected and safe existence.

This schism of dual selves is amplified in the army, where Tae-yul must be sure to divide his two conflicting roles (Japanese soldier and Korean resistance fighter), and must even sign his legal documents with two names: "We have to sign both our names—Japanese and Korean: Japanese because we're citizens of the Empire, Korean so they can keep track of us, of the ones who aren't really Japanese" (149). Just like Tae-yul is pretending to serve the Japanese army, the Japanese army is pretending to serve Korea, but both sides are withholding the truth about their intentions.

Tae-yul's letters epitomize the struggle of restriction: from speaking out but learning how to navigate barriers of communication to reach an intended audience. A character who once resisted education and school—preferring instead the use of his hands for technical skills—he has shifted his approach and learned the value of the mind over the body. This, like many other moments in this text, prove how malleable and resourceful communities become during times of distress.

Chapters 26-29

Chapter 26 Summary: "Tae-yul"

Tae-yul is excelling in training. He is physically fit and mentally strong. However, he worries about what war will be like once he must actually kill US soldiers—who, ironically, are fighting to free Korea. He receives the package from home, but soldiers searched all of the contents and stole the food. Still, he enjoys the notes from his family, and nearly cries after Abuji's simple message of thanks. Back on duty, Tae-yul's unit must serve meals to the commanding officers—a rotating duty for all trainees. During dinner, he overhears the officers talking about a secret mission that involves Korean recruits. Tae-yul smiles, knowing that he is doing exactly what Sun-hee has done for so long when cleaning the table for him, Uncle, and Abuji. The next day, the commander asks the Korean unit for volunteers to go on a mission of "ultimate sacrifice" (164). Tae-yul confidently offers his loyalty, and impresses everyone.

Chapter 27 Summary: "Sun-hee"

The family receives a second letter from Tae-yul. He writes concisely, vaguely mentioning that the Emperor has selected him for an important mission that will utilize his previous experience in the "Japanese Youth Air Corps." Sun-hee thinks about it, and after reading between the lines, guesses that Tae-yul is training to become a kamikaze pilot. She hopes she is wrong and remembers how she overreacted with Uncle's situation by misreading Tomo's message. She reasons that if he were to actually become a pilot, it would extend his training period and that the war might end before he could actually fly; the thought of this relieves her.

After much deliberation, she shares her realization with Abuji. He listens intently to her concerns as she explains Tae-yul's extensive fascination with planes, kamikazes, and other clues that informed her understanding of the letter. He believes her, and together they wonder what to do next. Sun-hee finally suggests telling the Japanese authorities not to let him fly because they cannot trust the nephew of a resistance member. She hopes that this will prevent her brother from sacrificing himself. But Abuji explains how if they reveal Tae-yul's dangerous intentions, the Japanese will most likely execute him, therefore ruining her plan. They agree to think about it more. The next day after school, Sun-hee eagerly awaits her father. When he arrives, he tells her that he has informed the Japanese authorities.

Chapter 28 Summary: "Tae-yul"

Tae-yul's excitement of becoming a pilot quickly diminishes when he realizes the implications of being a kamikaze. The night before he ships off to Japan, he can't sleep. Tae-yul comes up with a plan while continuing to train, but doesn't yet reveal it. He is excited when he begins to learn more about the planes and enjoys his practical training. He admires the mechanics, even though they are a "lower class" of soldiers that the other pilots ignore (178). After numerous exercises for training, Tae-yul is surprised when the commanding officer addresses the cadets to inform them that Japan is losing the war, and that they are ready to practice flying real planes. Tae-yul's experience with gliders went well, and he is confident and excited about flying an actual plane—something he has only previously seen. His first experience goes better than he expected, and he loves to fly.

The kamikaze training is demanding, and involves the practice of flying into a target with eyes closed. Finally, the officers announce each pilot's mission. Tae-yul hopes he receives an assignment as a bomber, since some cadets become engineers or mechanics. He is relieved to see himself as a bomber, just as he had planned. But as he writes his last letter to his family—which the Japanese army claims will be completely uncensored—he begins to feel sadness for his family. He hopes his Uncle will know about his true purpose of joining the Japanese army. He signs off with his Korean name, rather than "Kaneyama Nobuo." The next morning, his commanding officer gives the final instructions, and after a ceremonial process, they board their planes and take off.

Chapter 29 Summary: "Sun-hee"

Sun-hee is tense from uncertainty and apprehension. The family has waited weeks for Tae-yul's outcome. Finally, they receive the bad news: an honorable death. Omoni cries uncontrollably and Sun-hee rushes to console her. Japanese soldiers deliver the message in a box with Tae-yul's final words and a symbolic sword. The box reads, "To the family of the late Kaneyama Nobuo" (192). Sun-hee can't believe it, but she keeps her composure herself and informs Abuji, who is quietly devastated. They all sit together in the main room, looking lifeless.

Sun-hee realizes the letter is two weeks old and tries to recall how she has spent her time since then. She is dazed and for days cannot function normally. Omoni is in deep mourning and unable to be in public during this time. Suddenly, a neighborhood accounting takes place. Sun-hee is the only representative for her family. But she is surprised when the soldiers make an announcement in Korean. It has never happened before. She quickly realizes, "The war was over. The Emperor had surrendered to the United States. Korea was free" (196). The neighborhood begins to celebrate, but Sun-hee is paralyzed thinking about how Tae-yul died two months before the war ended. She sits down to gather herself, and the widow, Mrs. Ahn, is the first person to console her.

Chapters 26-29 Analysis

The diminishment and dehumanization of Koreans continues, even in the army. This provides an impetus for Tae-yul's decision to demonstrate courage for not only himself, but his nation. Tae-yul's choices reflect his desire for Japan to respect Korea, and he becomes a symbol for Korean pride and resistance in a way that his Uncle never envisioned: by becoming a kamikaze. But he has ulterior motives, something he learned from observing Uncle operate as a shop owner under the guise of being chin-il-pa in order to tactically position himself for a greater purpose.

Though Tae-yul has placed himself in a dangerous situation, he seems to have a secret mission, perhaps one that the Japanese are not expecting—similar to how his Uncle taught him. His "act" as a soldier continues to deceive his Japanese officers just as Japan's Empire continues to deceive the Korean people (161). This inversion of power shows how characters must be flexible in desperate circumstances in order to combat their suppression. Though it seems that Tae-yul has flown to his death, there are foreshadows and clues that perhaps he is planning something else. It's unclear, but there is hope. In this way, the narrative emulates the secretive coded language that the characters must use to survive their environment; they aren't always able to say what they really want, and the audience must sometimes read between the words like Sun-hee deciphering letters from her brother (144).

Still, there is sadness in Tae-yul's actions. Perhaps the most revealing moment is when he confronts his potential fate and realizes he might never see his family, nor create his own. The harsh reality of a young man's life cut short sinks in, and the reader witnesses an innocent teenager coming to terms with the possibility of his own death:

> Then I think about other things. Girls. I've never had
> a girlfriend. Hee-wo, Jung-shin's older sister—I wish
> I could have gotten to know her better. Maybe we
> could have talked about things, about her family
> being chin-il-pa, about me joining the army, how life
> gets so complicated sometimes. Now the simplest
> things seem the best. Marriage, a family of my own,
> children. I never thought before about being a
> father—it seemed too far in the future (160).

Tae-yul's maturity and growth in the face of adversity underscores his character's evolution and sense of community. He is thinking of fatherhood, and being the head of his own family, just as his father raised him in the world. Though he struggles to express himself fully—most likely a result of being a young male raised under violent occupation—it is clear that his tone is appreciative and thankful for his family. What he cannot say in words, he says in his actions and in his sacrifice. Though mostly indirect, he tries to reassure and comfort his family's worries. In his potentially final moments, he gains ultimate agency by giving them his life under his own will, an act that he considers to be a privilege: "My last gift to you all is the knowledge that I have chosen the way of my death, which is something few of us are privileged to do" (195). For many, this would seem like a horrible fate, but for Tae-yul it is an honorable and autonomous choice that will benefit his family because they will gain honor and support from the Japanese Empire as a result of Tae-yul's service.

The theme of community in the face of struggle emerges as a critical element as the story progresses. Nearing the end, the family overcomes any of their differences and begin to appreciate one another like never before. But their love and unity extends beyond blood relatives, evidence that their community is more than just a single household, but an entire neighborhood, an entire nation. This camaraderie appears in small and large ways, like when Tae-yul becomes a pilot and his fellow Korean soldiers salute him as both a joke and an honor. Or, like when Sun-hee functions as the emotional support for her parents when they can't comprehend the reported death of their son. Or, when Mrs. Ahn is there to pick Sun-hee off the floor when she cannot overcome her grief. In the closing image of Chapter 29, every Korean comes out to celebrate, leaving behind their fears that they previously kept hidden indoors and joining the community they have been—and will continue to be—a part of before, during, and after the war. A rare moment of celebration, Korean pride, and unity flourishes at the news of the Japanese army's defeat:

> Suddenly, everyone around me was shouting, throwing their arms in the air, hugging one another, laughing, crying. A man grabbed the megaphone and began singing in Korean; most of the crowd joined in. People who had not been at the accounting came out of their houses to find out what was going on and quickly joined the raucous celebration (196).

Chapters 30-32

Chapter 30 Summary: "Sun-hee"

The war has ended, yet strangely, there is more violence and unrest in Korea as a result. The Koreans have started to retaliate against the Japanese for their decades of abusive occupation, and the Japanese are fighting back, while the American forces try to keep the peace. Sun-hee cannot go outside due to the chaos, so she waits indoors and observes the US soldiers and their oddly different features. Abuji brings back a package of rations provided by their military and it includes rice, gum, and other treats that the family enjoys. They've never had gum, and the experience of chewing it baffles them.

Sun-hee learns that the US soldiers are evacuating the Japanese, so decides to visit her friend Tomo. He is surprised to see her, and calls her Keoko—her Japanese name—though she isn't used to hearing it since the war ended. She worries about him and his family since they have to start a new life in a country where Tomo has practically never been. She gives him the stone from the night when Tomo stopped by to warn her about the metal raid. When Tomo mentions his condolences about Tae-yul's death, she freezes, since no one in her household talks about it. She wishes him safe travels, and returns home.

A month after the war ends, an American soldier delivers a package to the family's residence. Sun-hee eagerly awaits until her father returns to open it. When he arrives, he opens it and calls the remaining family together. Miss Lim, a woman in the community who Abuji has only met once, writes that she worked as a leader in the resistance and knew Uncle. Though she is uncertain of Uncle's exact situation, she believes he is in Manchuria but unable to return due to Communist uprisings in the north. The letter also mentions that Mrs. Ahn, the next door widow, helped many resistance members hide in a secret basement in her garden—this included Uncle before he left. Sun-hee is shocked and saddened by the news of Uncle but happy about Mrs. Ahn's underground involvement. Life slowly resumes for Sun-hee. She reads a newspaper from Abuji about the importance of kanji and scholarship. She helps Omoni weed in the garden. One morning, US soldiers are at the front gate honking their Jeep, then roar off. Omoni goes to see what is happening. She lets out a scream. Sun-hee goes to see what is wrong and sees Tae-yul, whom they thought dead.

Chapter 31 Summary: "Tae-yul"

Upon his return, Tae-yul eats a big meal and takes a long bath. The family patiently waits for him and gathers to talk late at night about his experience. He tells them what it was like to write his letter of decease and how they cancelled mid-flight because of heavy weather problems. While flying, Tae-yul admits he had a plan to purposely miss the US targets but knew that since the pilots had to return to base (due to weather), he would not have a chance to follow through. When they landed, the Japanese army put the pilots in jail for not completing their mission. They sat there for weeks without explanation until their release when the war ended. Tae-yul apologizes formally to his family for the pain he has caused.

Abuji begins to cry, saying Tae-yul does not need to apologize, and they continue listening to Tae-yul's stories. He withholds what prison was like, and how he is worried about his future. He doesn't know what he'll do now. He doesn't feel like a student anymore and is older, with more experience. While adjusting back to civilian life, he helps his father clean up and prepare the school. Abuji finds an article that Uncle published before the war, accusing Japanese leadership at the time. He comments on Uncle's courage. Tae-yul suddenly bursts out in anger and questions his father, asking "What right do you have to speak of courage?" (214). He storms out. He believes his father is a "coward" (215). It pains him to think of his family this way. He questions his own value as a man and regrets having failed his mission.

When he returns home at midnight, Sun-hee challenges him. Tae-yul tells her Abuji is a coward, a "worm burrowing into the ground...hoping all the bad things would go away! How can I respect such a man?" (217). She disagrees. She tells him that she believes Abuji was writing for the resistance newspaper but withholding his name to protect the family. She shows Tae-yul the article about education that Abuji had given her earlier that week. She thinks their father wrote it. Tae-yul is surprised, and starts to believe her. They deduce that Abuji had been writing against Japanese Imperialism the whole time, and that he was in danger each night the military came to check their house. Tae-yul can't believe how his father would have never mentioned anything to him, but Sun-hee assures him it was for the family's protection. Tae-yul grasps this truth and begins to cry.

Chapter 32 Summary: "Sun-hee"

When Tae-yul gets up early, Sun-hee follows after him. They talk about Uncle's shop, which remains abandoned. Abuji kept it in case Uncle returns. Sun-hee suggests that Tae-yul can be involved in restoring it. Tae-yul is excited and thinks he should reopen the press. Even without Uncle, he had learned some of the printing techniques from him. Tae-yul and Sun-hee imagine a new name for the business: "Printing—Kim Young-chun" (220), in honor of Uncle's Korean name. Sun-hee realizes that she must teach Tae-yul how to write properly since he will be a printer. She jokes, "'You'll be a terrible printer if you don't know how to read and write,' I said in a stern voice. But I couldn't keep the smile from my eyes" (220), and sits with him to teach him how to spell. She writes the first three letters of the Korean alphabet for him, and watches as Tae-yul begins to practice.

Chapters 30-32 Analysis

For the first time in the narrative, the alternating narrator sequence between Sun-hee and Tae-yul changes. Instead of the usual Sun-hee/Tae-yul repetition, a Sun-hee chapter follows another Sun-hee account. Though seemingly arbitrary, it is a purposeful shift in the structural narrative, reinforcing the absence of Tae-yul after his reported death. Just like the news of his death leaves the family feeling absent and empty in their regular lives, his missing chapter leaves readers feeling a sense of loss and interruption in expectations. Just as Sun-hee and her parents never expected to lose their brother, readers never expected to lose out on Tae-yul's perspective, having grown so accustomed to his presence and voice in the novel. This break in the narrative is more than a stylistic choice, it is an enforcement of the thematic losses endured throughout the novel.

After Tae-yul's possible death and Uncle's disappearance, Sun-hee loses all of the optimism she has managed to build up during the war. Her sense of hope crashes whenever thinking about Tae-yul's plane crash. More than ever, the psychological and emotional burden of the war has knocked her down, and for the first time in the whole narrative, her character seems utterly defeated. Juxtaposed with the celebration of Korean victory after the US drops an atomic bomb on Hiroshima, Sun-hee is unable to express joy, instead saddened by her family's losses. It's a contrast to the imagery of happiness in her neighborhood at that moment, when even the hidden family members come outside to rejoice. The tone is bittersweet, exemplifying how even for many Korean families during Japanese occupation, even victory carries defeat. Yet, Sun-hee manages to regain her leadership and confidence with the help of community—another important theme in the story. Mrs. Ahn aids her in that moment. The narrative later reveals that Mrs. Ahn worked in a secret escape system for resistance fighters like Uncle, highlighting how even someone as unsuspecting as a lonely and ignored widow found a way to create and assist those in her community during an oppressive regime.

Tae-yul's return reveals more about the complexity of life and sacrifice during war. His return is a tremendous boost for the family's morale, yet he is still unhappy and unclear about his own future. Having lost the opportunity to study like a normal teenager—enlisting to train for battle and learning how to fly airplanes as a kamikaze instead—he feels as if he doesn't fit easily back into civilian society. This is an intentional look from the author into how soldiers suffer from post-war stress and how many simply cannot integrate back into regular living after training to kill enemies—one of the many negative outcomes from war. That said, as the family has shown strength and resilience throughout, Tae-yul is able to find purpose when he decides to take over Uncle's printing shop. Once again, Korean legacy, family, and community save a character from the traumatic effects of Japanese imperialism, allowing him to continue his Uncle's traditions. The symbolism of Korean pride, community, and language intersect as he chooses to use his Uncle's birth name, "Kim Young-chun," for the printing shop's reopening as a way to honor his family's past. This understanding of the past allows him to endure the pain of the present while envisioning a path for the future. It is at the core of this novel's message, and it's quite fitting to end with this moment.

But there's more to the story than the overarching themes suggest. Uncle and Tae-yul and Sun-hee each represent the courageous leaders who acted courageously in whatever ways that they could, even if forbidden or dangerous. But the beauty of the story is in the sheer variety of resistances that the Korean characters were able to develop, suggesting that there is more than one way to be heroic, and that heroes might not arise solely from individual efforts as much as they grow from community networks. Abuji is a clear example of this, as Park largely portrayed him as a silent and even "cowardly" man throughout the text, but his children later discover his involvement in the Korean resistance movement in a much more subtle and nameless way (217).

Though the story never confirms his involvement, it strongly suggests that he was writing articles for the resistance newspaper, which reflected his political and intellectual ideologies. The fact that his involvement is never known for sure is indicative of how many Koreans had to live in those years—not knowing who to trust, what to believe, or what was real. But in this case (just as with Mrs. Ahn) it seems likely that many community members—otherwise seen as uninvolved, unthreatening, or useless—like Abuji had secret involvements that they kept hidden for safety purposes. Up until the very end of the narrative, characters are still learning about themselves, about their parents, about their neighbors, and redefining what is possible.

In this sense, Tae-yul's faux resurrection is the perfect way to end *When My Name Was Keoko*. His return to himself, to his family, to his reality is a metaphor for how every community member is able to return—in some way—to who they are. Whether it's using their Korean name, revealing that they were involved in the resistance, or simply being able to live with their family members again, every character transforms individually and collectively to signal a new chapter in their nation's history. An often overlooked or forgotten perspective when discussing World War II, Linda Sue Park reminds readers that it wasn't only Jewish families who suffered at the hands of the Nazis during this time period, but many others around the world, including Asia. And just as the world has suffered from these tragic events, it has also learned how to regather and rebuild. In the closing pages, Sun-hee realizes this when she says, "Tae-yul had come back from the dead. That made it seem as if anything was possible. I felt myself start to smile" (220). Linda Sue Park implores sympathy and empathy with Sun-hee in this moment as she fleshes out a collective sense of wonder, hope, and possibility that hopefully increases after experiencing the worst.

CHARACTER ANALYSIS

Sun-hee (Keoko)

Sun-hee is in many ways the primary character, though she is not the only narrator. Her stories reveal the additional struggles of being under Japanese occupation as a young Korean girl. Because of gender expectations, her character develops differently and she must navigate other sets of complications that the male characters don't. From the onset, it's clear that Sun-hee is rebellious, aware, spirited, and inquisitive—defying her expected role as a quiet and subservient daughter. Her toughness and fearlessness are critical elements of the story and are often turning points for other characters, whose outcomes change because of Sun-hee's involvement (i.e. informing Uncle to flee). The contrast of her character's boldness increases due to the other Korean and Japanese schoolgirls she is around, who exhibit a fear and lack of control that only amplifies Sun-hee's strengths:

> Now some of the girls had tears rolling down their faces. Others moved their lips in silent prayer. The girl next to me had fallen over in a faint. Oddly, this made me feel stronger. I didn't want to faint; I wanted to be aware, to see what happened (109).

She will battle for her family, even in the face of threatening danger—a pride and resilience shown regularly throughout the narrative.

Tae-yul (Nobuo)

Unlike Sun-hee (often constrained by being the youngest and a daughter), Tae-yul's place in the family as the eldest and a son offers a different perspective. He is boldly expressive and given more responsibility in family business, often sitting with Uncle and Abuji at the table when discussing important matters. However, Tae-yul struggles to accept his father, Abuji, whom he views as weak and powerless. Instead, he follows in the footsteps of Uncle, who is involved in the underground Korean resistance. Tae-yul's admiration for Uncle leads him to join the Japanese Imperial Army, a risky decision that he hopes will yield glory and additional supplies for his family. This decision highlights how tactical and decisive Tae-yul is; he sees himself as a leader who needs to act for his family. Though a teenager, he sees himself as capable of being the man of the house, especially once Uncle flees for his safety. However, Park uses dramatic irony at the story's end to reveal how narrow-minded Tae-yul actually was, as he learns about his father's involvement in the Korean resistance as a covert writer. Tae-yul, therefore, represents a cautionary tale about learning how to perceive the strength of others not only for their traditional and obvious contributions, but for their subtle characteristics as well.

Uncle

In many ways the heroic archetype, Uncle is inspiring, a model of Korean pride and resistance, and joyfully passionate. His happiness and vigor for life represent the highest version of a Korean man during Japanese occupation. Though he is powerless against the Japanese Empire, he does not allow their tyranny to crush his spirit or his national ambition. Instead, he continues to find alternatives to express his people's culture and needs, running a print shop at night for the Korean resistance newspaper. The stories and experiences he shares with the two young narrators lay a groundwork for their subversive and prudent decision-making to aid the family. When Uncle flees, it represents a turning point in the novel, a milestone that marks the rising conflict for the family. His absence leaves a gaping hole that Tae-yul desperately tries to fill when he joins the army. Though the resolution does not clarify what becomes of Uncle—i.e. he never returns—readers remain in awe of his selflessness and bravery, and his resilient spirit endures through the children, and even through Abuji.

Abuji (Hyungnim)

Abuji represents the calm, collected, and academic father. He is level-headed, steady in demeanor, and analytically astute in his approach to his nation's crisis. As a local scholar and principal, he is a noble member of the community. However, he is also part of the Japanese system of oppression, since his school indoctrinates students into learning Japanese customs, history, and language. Though he is impotent against this, he doesn't seem to overtly challenge his people's oppression like Uncle. On the contrary, he watches while his son gets his bike taken by soldiers, and while soldiers burn his daughter's journal in front of everyone—never indicating any hint of resistance or anger. Tae-yul questions his father's character, and their relationship begins to deteriorate when Abuji cannot uphold the traditional strength of a man as his son believes he should. Tae-yul's explosive anger climaxes when he asks his father, "What right do you have to speak of courage?" (214) after the war. What Tae-yul fails to see, however, is that Abuji's hid his form of academic and patient resistance against the Japanese Empire in his subtle actions and community leadership, indicating that the strength of a person appears in various shapes and sizes—not always necessarily through force or battle.

Omoni

Omoni's character acts as a neutralizing force in the family, and she's a narrative balance. She seems peripheral because she is soft-spoken, but her love and strength arise in the most necessary moments, offering a quiet consistency amid the turmoil and chaos around her. Since her education is low, she does not speak Japanese, and because of this, she lacks the ability to access information at the same rate as even her own daughter. Therefore, Sun-hee often translates for her, which makes Omoni seem helpless. However, there are instances in the text when she stands up to the Japanese soldiers in ways that not even Uncle would, and these scenes show that she is more capable than we assume. She also looks out for her community, making sure to keep the widowed neighbor, Mrs. Ahn, safe during the military's "neighborhood accountings." As with each character, her unique personality is much deeper than the surface suggests; her silent but firm presence portrays yet another way that characters cope during crisis, once again proving that there is no singular way to respond to calamity.

Resistance and Liberation Occurs Differently for Every Individual

Throughout *My Name is Keoko*, Park portrays how a nation, a family, and individuals must respond to crisis and oppression in various forms of resistance. For some, their fight is literal, and they go to war and fight courageously for their family's well-being (Tae-yul). For others, it is subtle, and they fight using subversive underground tactics to dismantle the oppressor (Uncle). And for others, they don't seem to fight at all—yet even in their non-action, resistance manifests in unexpected ways (Abuji).

At the core of this novel, Park explores how individuals—when faced with the most challenging realities of life, death, loss, and abuse—must find ways to cope and endure by fighting. Yet fighting does not have to look the same for every individual. People should not expect a strong young man like Tae-yul, who is interested in plane mechanics, to respond to crises in the same way as an elder like Mrs. Ahn who can barely walk does—yet both must find ways to resist defeat. Whether mentally, spiritually, or physically, each character demonstrates a range of resisting occupation.

The most obvious and expected form of resistance is actual resistance by military force. Tae-yul decides to join the Japanese Imperial Army and later becomes involved as a kamikaze pilot. He believes that by sacrificing his life, his family will gain not only honor but, more importantly, will receive additional supplies from the Japanese. He uses his body more than his mind to fight against the oppressive Japanese forces. Though he has a plan to subvert the system, his plan eventually fails. He sits in jail—though his intentions fulfill their desired effect and his family receives more supplies and better treatment from the Japanese soldiers in Korea. In effect, Tae-yul tries to benefit from the system in place and responds by adapting to the system rather than trying to enact structural change.

Uncle also exhibits a traditional model of resistance during occupation. His involvement in the underground Korean resistance movement is, quite literally, a resistant act. But as opposed to Tae-yul, Uncle is operating within a network of resistance to try and overthrow the actual system itself. His involvement shows a community's ability to develop an evolved, calculated, and tactical response to oppression. Rather than allowing the Japanese forces to blindly destroy the Korean community, many Koreans make a unified effort to resist their erasure, giving men and women like Uncle (and Mrs. Ahn) a community purpose that may sometimes go unseen by others. When others see and acknowledge this type of resistance is perhaps the most powerful action as it imparts confidence, pride, and hope in the people: "What Uncle and others like him are doing— it's more important than anything. We aren't Japanese— we're Korean. But we'll never be allowed to truly be Korean unless we have our independence" (90).

On the other hand, resistance can also be a private or solitary act, a psychological or emotional space where a character can develop their internal defense against the sense of defeat. Sun-hee's journal takes on this purpose. Because she is a young girl who cannot enlist in the army or run a print shop, her ways of fighting back seem limited. She focuses her energy inward, and begins to master her sense of Korean heritage and pride through language and intellect. Though her body may be unable to express literal resistance against the Japanese soldiers, her mind becomes her fortress.

Inspired by Mrs. Ahn's act of refusing to learn the Japanese numeric system—claiming "They cannot have my thoughts. I will not allow it" (74)—Sun-hee begins to cherish her ideas, writing against the Japanese oppression in her notebook and secretly learning how to write and think like a subversive Korean. In many ways, her act of secret rebellion is the most threatening to Japanese control, because if they cannot force her into obeying their ideology, they will never control her. Due to her age and gender, this is the only way Sun-hee can resist, but it's effective for her and allows her to develop strength in ways that even the grown men in her community lack.

Each character, as a result of their oppression, finds a method of fighting, of resisting, of rejecting—and it looks different for all. However, it's important to note that in each instance, resistance also happens in response to a legacy of abuse. This highlights how, as members of any society, a community can only tolerate so much harassment, targeting, and dehumanization until that community decides to fight back:

> They're doing it again. Taking whatever they want.
> Grandfather's hair, Omoni's jewelry, Sun-hee's
> diary. My bicycle. And we can't do anything to stop
> them. Now it's Uncle they want. And they want me
> to stand there and do nothing again. This time, I have
> to do something (141).

Tae-yul's comment shows how his decision to fight back was a result of his family's and nation's lineage of abuse. In other words, a person or community's choice to be rebellious does not simply emerge overnight, but is a layered reaction in response to years and even generations of neglectful treatment.

Sacrifice and Struggle Deepens the Appreciation for Community

Essential to the physical or emotional survival of every character is community. Whether family, school, culture, neighborhood, or other types of sub-communities that exist, individuals need to have a sense of place in order to maintain joy, hope, and sense of self. In the narrative, community takes on many forms, and it's clear that as the struggles and sacrifices of the characters increase, so does the need for community.

Community is many things, but in the case of *When My Name Was Keoko,* it largely takes on a cultural and regional shape. Community is who one lives with and around, who one identifies as, and who one can trust. During war, these factors become less and less clear, so the sense of community shrinks, but in doing so, it also becomes tighter and more resilient. The ability to identify community in one individual during a time of chaos and danger is perhaps more powerful than being able to find community in hundreds during a time of peace and safety. In war, relationships develop a more defined purpose and urgency than ever before.

A clear example of concentrated community is when Mrs. Ahn, a widow previously shunned by her community during times of peace, becomes a symbol of community in times of war. Her relationship with Sun-hee and Omoni flourishes, as they develop a system of helping each other when needed. These parties—mere next door neighbors—would arguably never have established a community if soldiers were not constantly placing them in danger and threatening their sense of peace and safety. Thus, as they are more and more suppressed, they begin to look to each other for safety and a sense of comfort. This community yields large benefits for all—an exchange that resultantly benefits everyone involved. Mrs. Ahn is able to learn Japanese from Sun-hee and is alerted by family members when needed, and in return, Mrs. Ahn shares her rarest supplies with them and secretly houses Uncle when Japanese soldiers hunt him.

Through neglect and abuse, the Korean nation's sense of community grows and becomes stronger. More than anything, it lives in the people, and comes to light during times of darkness. As Sun-hee explains, her sense of love for her Korean community arises only when she faces the utmost danger:

> What did it mean to be Korean, when for all my life Korea had been part of Japan? It took the words of a man I'd never heard of—a faraway American—to make me realize something that had been inside me all along. Korean was the jokes and stories Uncle told us. It was the flag he'd drawn. It was the rose of Sharon tree Omoni had saved, and the little circle Tae-yul had carved on the bottom of the gourd bowls. Korean was the thoughts of Mrs. Ahn, in her own language, not someone else's (111).

Her own realization reveals just how often people take community for granted until forced to recognize it.

The Ability to Shift Morals and Expectations During War

Hinging on the ability to survive and endure a near-destructive experience is one's ability to shift and adapt morals and expectations during times of distress, particularly in war. Time and again, the novel reveals how characters must continually reshape their understanding of what's around them in order to survive. Whether it's learning who to trust, finding ways to tolerate an outcome, or allowing more flexibility in traditional gender roles, humans cannot remain static if they want to survive a crisis.

Besides the obvious violent dangers of an occupied nation during war, being able to adapt to new standards is among the most threatening realities that can challenge a person's survival. It appears throughout the narrative in each character's experience, as something that they once believed to be true is no longer applicable the following day, and they must elasticize themselves in order to endure and continue forward. One of the biggest ways this is show in the text is through the use of "chin-il-pa"—or Koreans who support Japanese. It's a derogatory term within the Korean community, used to signify anyone who betrays their people to gain Japanese favor, but as the story progresses, it's clear that the situation isn't as black and white as it may seem.

At times, Sun-hee despises chin-il-pa, but must reconsider her position when her Uncle—a proud Korean—becomes chin-il-pa in order to progress in his business. In moments like this, the characters must struggle with deep introspection, questioning what they once believed and trying to determine a new truth in response to an immediate and evolving context: "

> It's so confusing. Uncle acting like chin-il-pa when he's not...Tomo, the son of an important Japanese official, helping a resistance worker...Uncle disobeying Abuji in order to be able to obey him one day. If I can't fully understand, how can she? (90).

Here, Sun-hee grapples with her changing sense of reality. What she used to believe as true has morphed within the span of a few days, and she must continually regather her morals, beliefs, and expectations to fit a new circumstance. Her perception of truth is not rigid—she must learn how to accept and question former beliefs. It is an ability that allows her to cope with the changes and effects of war and violence, and one perhaps undervalued as a sign of strength and endurance.

Warfare and crisis, more than anything else, force individuals to question everything, and if one fails in reinterpreting surroundings, it may perhaps lead to a disconnect with family, community, and safety. The characters grapple with this and adapt their beliefs on a regular basis, having to make difficult choices that could lead to the survival of themselves, and their families. Decisions about culture, relationships, friendships, and loyalty arise, choices that define who they are as individuals. In doing so, these choices re-shift how they cope with their present. Sun-hee again must grapple with her choices while talking to Tae-yul about their father:

'More important than family?' she asks. But it's not one of her usual whiny little-sister questions. She's thinking hard, I can tell. 'Our duty to Abuji is important,' I say. 'It's a part of our culture. But if the Japanese have their way, someday there won't be any such thing as our culture. When Uncle works for independence, he works for the right to live as Abuji wants us to…Do you see what I mean?' (90).

Rarely is a child forced to choose between the expectations of her father and the ambition of her uncle, but this novel shows again and again how war places everyone in compromising situations of morality and expectation—and one's ability to choose may result in one's ability to live another day.

Korean Nationalism

Korean national symbols appear frequently throughout the text. From Uncle's lessons about Korean imagery, to references of Korean scriptures, to Omoni's Rose of Sharon tree, characters find ways to cultivate and embrace their Korean heritage in secrecy. Punishable by law, the Japanese have stripped away the Korean's sense of history—a tactic commonly used by oppressive forces who wish to demoralize a nation. The only way Koreans can maintain their sense of national pride during Japanese occupation is to teach the younger generations about it in informal and subversive ways.

Among these instances, Uncle teaches Sun-hee and Tae-yul about the Korean flag—which they have never seen before since it is illegal to display. Uncle draws it on paper while his young family members watch in awe and wonder, imagining they will one day see it flying above Korea. Uncle advises them, ""Keep it in your minds always—what the flag looks like and what it means" (23), insinuating that it's more than an image, but a source of pride and comfort. Afterwards, he must burn the paper so there is no evidence of his treason against the Emperor of Japan. Another time in which Korean symbolism is important is when Omoni must plant Japanese blossoms in her garden and must get rid of her Korean Rose of Sharon trees. Instead, she covertly keeps a tree in the back, in honor of her Korean family and name. It is literally a way for her—and her children—to nourish their roots in a time of need.

Coded Language

Because of Japanese oppression, the Korean community must develop secret modes of communication to express themselves without the consequences of military punishment. It takes form in both the private and public spheres, between family members and organized resistance movements. It blurs the lines of reality and trust, but also creates more avenues of possibility for those involved in the code. Coded language appears in Uncle's printing press in a literal sense—an underground newspaper to secretly inform the Korean resistance movement. But it also occurs in the actions of the people—in the coded interactions and networks of support. Mrs. Ahn's involvement in housing Korean runaways is also a form of coded language and exchange; those who are aware of her secret are able to participate and benefit, while those who aren't—such as the Japanese or chin-il-pa—are unaware and therefore unable to disrupt her communications.

The motif of coded language appears most notably at the end of the story when Tae-yul tells Sun-hee:

I'll be allowed to write letters, but I'm sure they'll be censored. I won't be able to put down the truth as I see it. I'm counting on you to read between my words and uncover their true meaning. It would mean a lot to me to know that you'll try to understand what I really want to say (144).

Knowing he cannot speak forwardly, he and Sun-hee must trust each other to decipher his words in a way that will "uncover their true meaning." Ultimately, in times of oppression and censorship, this recurring idea of communicating in a clandestine form underscores how resourceful people can be when silenced in order to maintain their authentic voice with loved ones.

Supervision/"Accounting"

To create a mood of discomfort in the story—much like the mood felt by those who lived during the Japanese occupation—there is a constant presence of supervision in the narrative. Soldiers constantly watch or listen to characters, and even their most private spaces—such as writing in a notebook inside one's bedroom at night—are no longer safe spaces. The Japanese presence is intrusive, infiltrating, and unwelcome, entering neighborhood homes, community businesses, and family privacy without warning. Japanese oppression becomes symbolized as a constant vigilance and distrust, creating tension and fear for the characters being "accounted." Even in schools, there are Japanese soldiers overlooking the young pupils and teachers, enforcing brute action and fear. The constant interruption of these soldiers creates an atmosphere of obedience—if not anger. There are countless examples in the text of this overwatch, some less subtle than others:

> Onishi-san was in the room. He was the man who served as the military attaché for our school [...] Onishi-san's job was to make sure all the students were learning to be good citizens of the Empire. He came into our classroom several times a week, often in the middle of a lesson (26-27).

This sign of control permeates the experience of the Korean characters, as they must learn to navigate the punishing eye of the Japanese Emperor. Even willing to interrupt a teacher mid-lesson, their presence is constant and ubiquitous.

IMPORTANT QUOTES

1. "I wasn't supposed to listen to men's business, but I couldn't help it. It wasn't really my fault. Ears don't close the way eyes do." (Chapter 1, Page 9)

   Though WWII and Japanese occupation is at the forefront of this story, there are also other "battles" happening in a cultural sense. In the first chapter, gender gaps and household divisions separate the characters from each other. Sun-hee—a girl and the youngest child—can only be a house cleaner while her brother, Tae-yul, can speak with the men. However, as Sun-hee's quote reveals, she doesn't easily conform to the social expectation and she inevitably finds ways to interact and gain information by listening in the background. It's an introduction to the intrepid nature and boundary-breaking attitude which defines her character in this novel.

2. "The person at the top had to be Japanese. The principal was the father of my friend Tomo. All our lessons were in Japanese. We studied Japanese language, culture, and history. School weren't allowed to teach Korean history or language. Hardly any books or newspapers were published in Korean. People weren't even supposed to tell old Korean folktales." (Chapter 1, Page 12)

   Japanese occupation and social conditioning is prominent in this narrative. In every situation, the Japanese have revoked Koreans of their status and power by relegating them to second-class citizens. As stated, Japanese "had to be" above the rest, therefore perpetuating their ability to keep the Koreans below them in every aspect. In addition, all schooling and education related to Japanese history and culture, blatantly negating Korean heritage as a way to strip the community of any unity or pride.

3. "'Why do we have to remember it? Why can't we just put the picture up on the wall? That way we'll see it every day and we'll always know what it looks like.' Uncle reaches out and pulls gently on one of her braids. 'We can't, little cricket. It is against the law to fly this flag—even to put up a picture of it. Korea is part of the Japanese Empire now. But someday this will be our own country once more. Your own country.'" (Chapter 4, Page 23)

    As part of controlling not only the body, but the mind and spirit as well, Japanese occupation did not allow Korean families to brandish any signs of their Korean nationality, including any imagery or symbols of their flag. It can only live in the memory of the elders—or those knowledgeable of it—and becomes a mythical idea that they must lock away in private. In this particular scene, Uncle is teaching the younger family members about the flag and why it's illegal. It is one of many examples in the text where the family must harbor their secret knowledge and a develop a sense of trust in their coded language in order to maintain their Korean identity.

4. "Onishi-san's job was to make sure all the students were learning to be good citizens of the Empire. He came into our classroom several times a week, often in the middle of a lesson. We always stopped what we were doing and bowed to him. Then he'd stand at the back of the room and observe us for a while. I could tell he made the teacher nervous. I tried especially hard to give the right answers when he was around." (Chapter 5, Page 25)

The repeating motif of Japanese supervision forms a pillar of fear, power, control, and oversight in the lives of the Korean characters.
They cannot freely express themselves, and must live under the vigilant eye of the Japanese military, or worse, Koreans who report against their fellow community members. The presence of their vigilance makes everyone uncomfortable, especially the educators who are responsible for shaping young minds to be indoctrinated during Japanese occupation. The mood is tense and violent.

5. "Chin-il-pa meant 'lover of Japan.' It was almost like a curse. Chin-il-pa were people who got rich because they cooperated with the Japanese government. I hadn't done anything like that! Why were they cursing me, calling me that awful name? I ran home, blinking away tears." (Chapter 5, Page 32)

Perhaps the only thing more despised within the Korean community besides the Japanese soldiers are "chin-il-pa." These are Korean nationals who have sold out and "cooperate with the Japanese government" to save their own skin. Often exposing their fellow Koreans, it creates an environment of uncertainty and distrust. No one knows who they can share information with, because they might trade that information for Japanese favor. In this quote, Sun-hee faces persecution from her Korean classmates for her ability to speak Japanese fluently. Her horror of others identifying her as chin-il-pa reveals how much internalized shame and guilt the epithet carries for Koreans.

6. "I said nothing. I could hardly believe we were cooking animal food for our dinner." (Chapter 7, Page 42)

Times were never easy for Korean families during Japanese occupation, but they quickly grow worse when the war begins. The imagery of human desperation and dehumanization reaches a disturbing zenith when the family must resort to eating animal feed for dinner. This act symbolizes how not only one family, but the entire Korean nation was no longer valued as equal citizens but as animals who ate what pigs and cows ate.

7. "Truly, rose of Sharon trees are not as beautiful as cherry trees. But if that little tree were ever planted outside again, I knew it would be the most beautiful tree in the world." (Chapter 7, Page 46)

The rose of Sharon trees emerge as a strong national symbol for Koreans. When Japanese soldiers order everyone to cut their trees down and plant Japanese cherry blossoms in their place, Omoni keeps one of her Korean trees and plants it in a secret location. Sun-hee imagines a future when her country and people regain independence and how hopeful and beautiful their national tree will look. She is still hesitant, however, saying "if" rather than when, indicating how low the morale of the Korean people had sunk.

8. "Uncle becoming chin-il-pa—is this what worries Abuji? The chin-il-pa do everything they can to please the Japanese. Patriotic Koreans—those who work for independence from Japan—hate the chin-il-pa. Sometimes the patriots wreck shops and homes. There are rumors that chin-il-pa get beaten, even killed. Abuji's face always goes dark when he hears those rumors. Koreans killing Koreans, he once said—it's worse than anything the Japanese can do to us." (Chapter 8, Page 53)

While shedding light on the negative stigma associated with chin-il-pa, Abuji's fears begin to show. As an educated and well-tempered scholar, he cannot fathom Koreans persecuting their own people. Knowing that his brother is secretly involved in the illegal Korean resistance only amplifies his fears and concerns. It is in these situations that characters must grapple with their daily worries and find ways to survive not only the threat of Imperial Japanese abuse, but the threat of each other as well. Once again, Linda Sue Park shows how others battles took place apart from the actual war.

9. "So much good news—for the Japanese...It's so odd. The war is going well for the Japanese—which makes life better for Koreans too. If the Japanese win the war, will things be better still?" (Chapter 10, Page 67)

   Ironically, improvement and success for Japan early in the war translates into improvement and success for Korea. Since Japan controls Korea during the war, it is in Korea's interest to stay informed of Japan's actions and potentially benefit from their victories. Though they won't ever experience the same level of treatment as their Asian counterparts, there is some potential hope in seeing changes as a result of Japanese victory. Yet, as the story progresses, Sun-hee realizes that the US Army wants to liberate Korea by defeating Japan, and it later becomes clear to her that it is Korea's dream to see Japan finally defeated.

10. "'But, Ajima, you have only learned to count to five. Surely we should continue, to ten—' There were ten households in our association; she would need to be able to count at least that high. 'No.' Mrs. Ahn's voice rang out strongly. I looked at her, surprised. 'No,' she

said again. She lowered her voice a little. 'I will tell you why. I have nothing in this world—you know that. Everyone knows that. No children, no family. Alone here all day with nothing but my thoughts.' Her voice was still fierce as she continued, 'They cannot have my thoughts. I will not allow it.'" (Chapter 11, Page 73)

In a powerful and inspiring scene, the widowed neighbor, Mrs. Ahn, refuses to learn Japanese numbers. Though it threatens her safety and wellbeing (since she has to count to 10 in Japanese during the neighborhood accountings), she simply refuses to give her body and mind to Japanese occupation. It is her mental and spiritual form of resistance, since she has nothing else left for the Japanese to take. She is alone, yet maintains hope and a sense of self and pride that is admirable for a character with nothing to celebrate.

11. "But I don't feel like playing anymore—all because of that stupid announcement. 'Express your gratitude,' they'd said. What they take: our rice, our language, our names. What they give: little rubber balls. I can't feel grateful about such a bad deal." (Chapter 12, Page 76)

As Tae-yul grows older and more aware, he begins to see the inconsistencies and contradictions from the Japanese leaders. They take everything from the Koreans, but still expect the Koreans to show love and admiration towards their oppressors. Tae-yul's realization occurs after students receive small rubber balls as toys to celebrate a Japanese victory in a rubber-producing region of the Pacific; the toy is a symbol of Japanese expansion. While the children are playing, soldiers stop them and make the students recite a pledge of allegiance to "express gratitude." Afterwards, Tae-yul goes home instead of staying with his friends, angry at the Japanese's insolence.

12. "What Uncle and others like him are doing—it's more important than anything. We aren't Japanese—we're Korean. But we'll never be allowed to truly be Korean unless we have our independence." (Chapter 14, Page 90)

Resistance takes shape in many ways throughout the text, depending on the character and their strengths or limitations. In the case of Uncle, he utilizes his status as a respectable male printer in the community and leverages his shop to run an underground newspaper for Korean rebels. His pride and actions are infectious, especially for Tae-yul, who heralds him as the example of manhood in their household. The desire for complete liberation appears in the hearts and minds of the Koreans by men like Uncle waging a secret battle on the frontlines.

13. "'More important than family?' she asks. But it's not one of her usual whiny little-sister questions. She's thinking hard, I can tell. 'Our duty to Abuji is important,' I say. 'It's a part of our culture. But if the Japanese have their way, someday there won't be any such thing as our culture. When Uncle works for independence, he works for the right to live as Abuji wants us to...Do you see what I mean?'" (Chapter 14, Page 90)

Morals and family expectations constantly shift in times of war and distress. Sun-hee, in particular, finds herself continually redefining her place and purpose, and must wrestle with enormous decisions as a child. In response to Tae-yul's adoration of Uncle, she questions whether she should also disobey her father or follow the cultural family code that she has known all her life—even if her father isn't showing signs of obvious leadership. It presents a conflict of interest for her, as she must choose between family traditions, cultural morals, or Korean independence. This internal dispute is a larger theme that all characters in the text must deal with in overcoming the war.

14. "That was what Tomo had been talking about. He'd been warning me that our metal things were about to be taken away. Maybe he thought that if we knew in advance, we could hide some things before it happened. But telling me straight out would have made him a traitor to the Japanese, his own people. He'd been telling me the only way he could—and I hadn't understood." (Chapter 15, Page 94)

Since Koreans don't have freedom of expression during Japanese occupation, they must communicate in coded language. This creates the problem of miscommunication, distrust, and anxiety. When Tomo—a Japanese friend of Sun-hee—tries to inform her about potential danger, she misreads his message and further endangers her Uncle as a result, telling him to flee. It's one of the various barriers that the Korean community had to deal with during occupation: how to share messages and inform each other of danger without tipping off the authorities or unintentionally worsening their own situation.

15. "I didn't expect this. I thought we'd be supervised by our teachers. The soldiers are a lot crueler. Punishment isn't being struck with a bamboo cane across your legs but standing with the shovel held over your head. For a long time—hours, even. Some students get slapped

hard in the face for working too slowly or not saluting respectfully enough." (Chapter 16, Page 104)

Even when Tae-yul and other young Koreans want to learn and play a role in the country, they face subhuman treatment. In this situation, young Koreans had volunteered to help build an airstrip outside of town. In many cases it represented a way to keep busy and contribute their efforts to a larger purpose. However, as the stinging language of the passage reveals, the Korean student volunteers suffered beatings, abuse, punishment, often disciplined worse than usual. It's evidence of the lack of opportunities given to the Koreans, but also how even in trying to pursue a skill they faced mistreatment.

16. "Too many eyes. I understood this. The Japanese were watching us because of Uncle's escape. Not as closely as during the first few weeks, but still more than usual. We might be studying Hangul and soldiers might burst in on us. It was too dangerous. I promise one day…One day? When? When would the Japanese let us have our own language back?" (Chapter 17, Page 112)

There are literal and figurative dangers for every Korean character in this historically-based novel, due to tyrannical Japanese supervision. So much so that Abuji will not even consider teaching Sun-hee the Korean language, Hangul, in their own home for fear of punishment. The suppression of Korean culture and language is evident, but this represents the highest loss for the people—not even allowed to speak their own language in their own homes without persecution.

17. "Those soldiers tonight, tearing apart our house. And me? I'd stood there, frozen. I hadn't done anything—I

hadn't even said anything. And I'm three years older than Abuji was then. I know now. What could he have done? What could any of us do?" (Chapter 18, Page 124)

In a rare instance of empathy, Tae-yul begins to understand his father's—as well as his own—futility in the face of Japanese Imperialism. After hearing the brutal story about his grandfather's mistreatment from Japanese soldiers, Tae-yul wondered why his father did nothing to stop them. But now that Tae-yul's father and family have faced disrespect, Tae-yul must grapple with his powerlessness. It reveals a legacy of abuse that has gone on for generations, and the story creates a bridge between the elders and youth in how they both suffer equally. Coming to terms with this reality, Tae-yul represents the younger generation learning how their parents must have felt in past decades, and forgiveness becomes possible.

18. "But do not forget, Sun-hee—they burn the paper, not the words [...] it was important. Our stories, our names, our alphabet. Even Uncle's newspaper. It was all about words. If words weren't important, they wouldn't try so hard to take them away." (Chapter 19, Pages 125-26)

The power of voice and language is perhaps the biggest pillar of resistance and liberation for the Korean community. By eliminating these practices, the Japanese hope to stifle the Korean spirit. However, many of the characters find alternative ways to preserve their tongues, minds, spirits. Knowing the importance of this, Tae-yul reminds his sister of how valuable their ability to express is. From Uncle's underground newspaper to speaking Korean in the house, the Japanese ironically fear the Korean voice, and do everything they can to disable and eliminate it. This leads to the coding of Korean identity, which the characters achieve by various covert means.

19. "It was so cruel. All of it—the occupation, the war, Uncle in hiding, Tae-yul going into the army...I needed to get out of that room; the unfairness of it all was choking me. I whirled and bolted out of the house." (Chapter 21, Page 136)

Sun-hee is a resilient and bold character. Yet even she collapses near the end of the story in sadness, feeling overwhelmed by the amount of loss and pain suffered from the war. Her trauma is deep, and she and her Korean community have suffered extreme cruelty for no apparent reason. When Tae-yul leaves after Uncle's disappearance, her house feels emptier—she feels emptier. The imagery of choking underscores not only the psychological, but physical impact of war on a person. The suffocating pressure of her situation is crushing, and she must run away from it in this rare moment of retreat.

20. "We have to sign both our names—Japanese and Korean: Japanese because we're citizens of the Empire, Korean so they can keep track of us, of the ones who aren't really Japanese." (Chapter 24, Page 149)

One of the most interesting elements of this history is how Koreans had two names, and essentially, two identities: as authentic Koreans, and as false Japanese. It's a cultural and political schism that prevents them from ever being complete. They must always operate as two halves, torn and in disagreement. The illusion of their Japanese citizenship is merely surface-level; the Japanese benefit from the Koreans being only partial

*citizens. Therefore, despite having legally-imposed
Japanese names, they must always reveal their Korean
names so that the Japanese can stratify them as lower
members, even in the military when they are sacrificing
their lives for the Japanese. Even in approaching their
deaths, they are seen as less than the Japanese.*

21. "Abuji never once interrupted me. He listened intently
    to every word. He didn't shake his head or act like I
    was crazy. I was grateful for that." (Chapter 27, Page
    171)

    *Abuji proves to be a kind, compassionate, and
    intelligent man. This is crucial to Sun-hee's
    development as an astute, confident, and studious
    young girl. Unlike other male members of her society,
    Abuji shows great respect and deeply values his
    daughter's contributions and ideas. It represents how
    gender roles have shifted in the house, especially with
    the absence of Tae-yul while he is at war. It speaks to
    how expectations and treatment shifts during extreme
    times. Even though Abuji has always valued his
    daughter's mind, he focuses on it even more when
    desperation ravages his family.*

22. "Then I think about other things. Girls. I've never had a
    girlfriend. Hee-won, Jung-shin's older sister—I wish I
    could have gotten to know her better. Maybe we could
    have talked about things, about her family being chin-
    il-pa, about me joining the army, how life gets so
    complicated sometimes. Now the simplest things seem
    the best. Marriage, a family of my own, children. I
    never thought before about being a father—it seemed
    too far in the future." (Chapter 28, Page 187)

    There is significant loss in this text, in this history.

However, some of the smaller losses of innocence become overshadowed by the larger ravages of war. In this quote, before Tae-yul's probable death as a kamikaze pilot, a sad moment of realization and tenderness for a young teenager who has never been able to live as a teenager arises. His boyish innocence is at the forefront, as he confesses his thoughts for "girls." Loss affects his life in more than one way, both literally and emotionally Even if he survives the war, he will never regain his youth, and his experiences of joy and love as a boy will forever be stolen from him and many Korean boys of his generation.

23. "A bit at a time we pieced together what had happened. The Americans had dropped two bombs on Japan. The bombs were said to have been powerful enough to destroy half a city. At first no one could believe this. Half a neighborhood, perhaps? Or half a major military base? But Abuji eventually confirmed that half of the city of Hiroshima had indeed been destroyed on August 6, and half of Nagasaki three days later." (Chapter 30, Page 198)

Much of this history revolves around a lack of information, disrupted communication, and censorship of Korean expression. Even at the end of the war, when Korea is now free from Japan, there is limited access to clear information. Abuji must "piece together" various news sources to "eventually confirm" what happened to end the war. Partially the result of war's chaos, partially the result of Japanese secrecy, this moment emblematizes how an environment of unreliable, inconsistent, and untruthful news has trapped the Korean community.

24. "Funny how the war made ordinary things seem special again." (Chapter 31, Page 214)

Hope endures throughout the text, but only in small ways. Here, Tae-yul is learning to cherish the "ordinary things" in his life again, such as sitting at a dinner table with his family and eating a real meal. It's a minor bright spot in an otherwise gloomy reality— knowing that everything one once took for granted is actually a wonderful privilege. It reminds readers to embrace and appreciate comforts, because during war or crises, they might experience the inhumanity of living in a dysfunctional or even persecutory world.

25. "The war had changed so many things. Uncle gone, Tomo gone. Jung-shin gone, too. Her family had left town immediately after the Japanese surrender, because anyone who had helped the Japanese was in as much danger as the Japanese themselves—more, maybe. I didn't know where they'd gone; I didn't even have a chance to say goodbye to her. I hoped with all my heart that she would write to me one day and let me know she was safe somewhere." (Chapter 32, Page 218)

The uncertainty of war leaves a trauma that no heart or soul can completely heal. Despite maintaining hope, resisting oppression, developing coded pathways of communication, and deepening community, war ultimately destroys a nation's morale and strips citizens of beauty, opportunity, and even life itself. In the final pages, Sun-hee reflects on how her Japanese and chin- il-pa friends are ironically now in danger in the way she and her family have been for decades. Yet she doesn't resent them. She grieves for them, wondering how they will manage in the years to come. Her sense of compassion and empathy is high since she has endured the trauma of war and persecution. Ending on this note leaves readers feeling the scars of what Korean—and even Japanese—families had to survive and overcome for so long. Their uncertainty and anxiety doesn't end when the war does.

ESSAY TOPICS

1. What does the loss of Korean names at the start of the novel represent? Why do you think the author chose to begin the narrative with this symbolic act? How does it shape the tone and arc of the narrative to have characters with two names?

2. Abuji's silence and composure in response to Japanese occupation is in direct contrast to Uncle's bold involvement in the Korean resistance. What are the pros and cons of each of these men's approaches? How does the family benefit from each male's response? How does the family suffer from each of their decisions?

3. Define Korean community in this novel. What does it look like? How does it form during times of oppression? What defines a member of the community? Why is it essential for each character to find this community and what role does it play for them?

4. There are many references of coded language in this novel. Identify three examples when characters must speak secretly. When and why does it happen? What causes them to code switch and how do they code their language? What are the effects of this coded communication? Does it benefit or hurt the characters involved?

5. Why is the Japanese Imperial Army so adamant about enforcing Japanese culture upon the Korean population? Why do they not allow Korean families to learn about their own history or keep their national symbols? Explain a moment in the story when this happens. Provide context and determine how it affects the characters' identities.

6. Sun-hee's journal nearly gets her family punished, yet she refuses to quit writing. Go back and re-read her journal entries. Choose one and analyze what it reveals about Sun-hee's character: Why is Sun-hee's journal so important for her? How does it empower her, specifically as a young Korean female? What does she reveal in the entry?

7. What does Mrs. Ahn's refusal to learn Japanese numbers indicate about her character? Why doesn't she simply learn Japan's number system so that she can be accounted for without the risk of punishment? Does her strategy work?

8. "What did it mean to be Korean, when for all my life Korea had been part of Japan?" (8). This quote illuminates the contradiction of living in your country while under foreign occupation. Choose one major character and compare/contrast how they deal with the issue of national, political, and cultural allegiance to both Korea and Japan. What drives them to show their loyalty to each nation and how do they display their accordance with each?

9. How does learning about Abuji's involvement in the resistance newspaper at the end of the novel influence the way you understood his character? Why do you think Linda Sue Park decided to inform the family and the readers about Abuji's subversive acts at the end of the book and not sooner in the story? What might this withheld revelation suggest about other characters in the novel?

10. What does the faux resurrection of Tae-yul symbolize for the entire Korean community in this book? How does the act of his perceived death (then returning to his

family after the war) represent a much larger message about the survival of Korean culture and history after Japanese occupation? Is this a hopeful or a misleading ending? Why?

Made in the USA
Monee, IL
10 July 2020